The Power of Coaching

Inspiring Untold Stories for Business Growth and Life Transformations

Volume 2

11 Amazing Coaches Share Stories and Strategies on How to Create Total Success in Many Areas of Business and Life

Compiled By Dr. Heather Tucker
CEO/Founder of www.AnotherLevelLiving.com

Get to Know the 11 Authors in this Book!

There's ONE Page online where you can access all the authors' websites and special offers from this book to make it super easy for you to follow up and connect with them further.

Go to **www.PowerofCoachingBook.com** right now before you forget. For a list of authors and their chapters, turn to the Table of Contents Page.

Enjoy the Book!

Sincerely,

Dr. Heather Tucker

Biz/Life Harmony Trainer, Coach, and Author to Entrepreneurs who want to Stress Less, Strengthen Relationships, and Lead with More Energy and Ease so that they can create Time, Money, and Emotional Freedom.

Copyright ©2024 by Dr. Heather Tucker and Another Level Living, Inc. All rights reserved. No part of this book or its associated ancillary materials may be reproduced or transmitted in any form, or by any means, electronic or mechanical, including photocopying, recording, or by any informational storage or retrieval system without permission from the publisher with the following exception: All authors within the book have the right to repurpose their own chapters in any way they choose to do so.

Published by Another Level Living, Inc., PO Box 64, Painter, VA 23420. (757) 656 – 1797 www.AnotherLevelLiving.com

DISCLAIMER AND/OR LEGAL NOTICES

While all attempts have been made to verify information provided in this book and its ancillary materials, neither the authors nor publisher assume any responsibility for errors, inaccuracies, or omissions and are not responsible for any financial loss by customers in any manner. Any slights of people or organizations are unintentional. If advice concerning legal, financial, accounting, or related matters is needed, the services of a qualified professional should be sought. This book and its associated ancillary materials, including verbal and written training, are not intended for use as a source of legal, financial, or accounting advice. You should be aware of the various laws governing business transactions or other business practices in your geographical location.

EARNINGS & INCOME DISCLAIMER

With respect to the reliability, accuracy, timeliness, usefulness, adequacy, completeness, and/or suitability of information provided in this book, Dr. Heather Tucker, Another Level Living, Inc., its partners, associates, affiliates, consultants, and/or presenters make no warranties, guarantees, representations, or claims of any kind. Readers' results will vary. All claims or representations as to income earnings are not to be considered average earnings. This book and all products and services are for educational and informational purposes only. Check with your accountant, attorney, or professional advisor before acting on this or any information. Dr. Heather Tucker and/or Another Level Living, Inc. is not responsible for the success or failure of your personal or professional decisions relating to any information presented by D. Heather Tucker, Another Level Living, Inc., or company products/services.

Any examples, stories, references, or case studies are for illustrative purposes only and should not be interpreted as testimonies and/or examples of what readers and/or consumers can generally expect from the information. Any statements, strategies, concepts, techniques, exercises, and ideas in the information, materials and/or seminar training offered are simply opinion and experience, and thus should not be misinterpreted as promises, typical results, or guarantees (expressed or implied).

ISBN: 979-8-9865070-1-9

PRINTED IN THE UNITED STATES OF AMERICA

Dedication

To those who may have difficulty finding their way, know that you are not alone and there is glory on the other side.

Your test is your testimony.

You are fearfully and wonderfully made and called for amazing things!

Enjoy reading this book because it was created with you in mind.

A special thank you to our family and friends who support our entrepreneurial endeavors. And a huge thank you to all the awesome authors of this book.

> *"Our deepest fear is not that we are inadequate. Our deepest fear is that we are powerful beyond measure."*
> -Marianne Williamson

Table of Contents

Introduction 1

Elevate Your Business & Life Chapters 3

Empowered To Shine
By Dr. Heather Tucker 4

Fine Tuning Your Performance
By Trish Carr 16

Unlock Your Potential
By Stephanie Richardson 26

Creating Magical Steps
By Sheryl Bernstein 37

Rocks in the River
By Lisa Birnesser 47

Guiding Leaders
By Joann Bellenkes 55

Elevate Your Life & Self Chapters 65

Turn Your Pain to Power
By Jewana White 66

It's Time For You
By Valerie J. Ritchie 76

Finding Your Authentic Self
By Susie Procini 86

A Paradigm Shift
By India Willis 95

Shining Your Light
By Alyssa Utecht 106

What's Next? 115

Introduction

This book, *The Power of Coaching, Vol. 2*, is for you if you are ready to achieve total success in your personal and professional development. In this book, you will read stories from business and life coaches who have successfully facilitated transformations and growth for others and their own lives. The purpose of this book is to highlight coaching as a solid avenue for reclaiming the power of your life through trust, truth, and transformation.

Coaching is an invaluable method for healing and positive change that too few people know about. We are here to make it more known. Coaching is available for anyone who chooses to invest in creating a brighter future for themselves and their loved ones. The beauty of coaching is that it bridges the gap from where one is to where they desire to be in any area of life. Too often, we can live our lives based on the terms of others and never fully step into our calling.

The 11 authors in this book share stories of hope and the possibility to shift any life into one filled with purpose, passion, and prosperity. Coaching can produce rapid, lasting results and change easily. These authors share their definition of coaching, testimonies of transformations that they facilitated and experienced for themselves, and key strategies they use to support others to take charge of their life journey. Through these stories, you will find that the benefits of coaching are priceless.

This book is divided into two sections. The first section includes chapters that focus on Business and Life Transformations. If you are a business owner, then you know that your business is an extension of all that you are, and these chapters will support you in your business and life growth.

The second section includes chapters that focus on Self and Life Transformation. These chapters were created for those seeking to become a better version of themselves and those around them. While reading this book, you might even be inspired and find that you have a calling to become a coach. Our company, Another Level Living Inc., teaches entrepreneurs the business of coaching and communication skills. We would be honored to support you on your journey.

It is our wish that you receive many nuggets of gold from these stories and are inspired to follow your true-life path.

Finally, the authors of this book want to hear from you! Each author has given a link to their website, where you can learn more about them and get their free gifts. Please take advantage of their offerings and reach out to connect with those who resonate with you.

Contact us if you have any questions about the authors, this book, Another Level Living Coaching Services, Certification Programs, or being a part of future books.

Elevate Your Business & Life Chapters

Empowered To Shine

By Dr. Heather Tucker

"The Cave You Fear to Enter Holds the Treasure that You Seek." ~Robert Campbell

Tell us about yourself, your expertise, and your coaching niche.

I am Dr. Heather Tucker, and I am a Biz/Life Harmony Trainer and Coach. I specialize in working with women entrepreneurs who have great responsibilities in their life (i.e., caregiving, health challenges, and relationship traumas) and/or have encountered great losses that are still impacting the present and clouding the future. These entrepreneurs may find themselves overwhelmed, stressed, anxious, and not getting the revenue results they desire and/or the deep-level aloha relationships they seek. The tug of war between love and money becomes a vicious cycle that creates a stressed mind and body and a heavy heart and energy.

I claim that it is possible to heal the past, live in the present, and joyfully walk into the future, regardless of what was. I also claim that it is 100% possible to receive your divine inheritance because you heard the call to entrepreneurship and acted. The Power of Emotional Intelligence (i.e., matters of the heart) and Effective Communication (i.e., matters of the mind) are literally the game changers when it comes to owning your power, standing in your greatness, and truly shining like the Light House Leader Queen that you are. All while knowing that other people's opinions and judgements of you are irrelevant because you know your value and royalty (Queendom).

I show how to create your ideal clarity, connection, organization, simplicity, and structure in your business to generate more revenue so that you can be more present and enjoy more time with your loved ones. It's possible to increase your calm, confidence, and cash flow by improving your energy, mindset, and emotional wisdom (heart space) so that can manifest the business and life you desire.

When you win your inner world, you master your outer world and your Freedom!

Tell us, what does coaching mean to you?

Coaching saves lives. Literally, coaching supports you in bridging the gap between where you and where you want to be and provides accountability as you make your goals and dreams a reality.

Coaching allows you to:

- Step out of your comfort zone, break free from the "terror barrier" resisting change, and guides you into the freedom that you seek.
- Step into your true empowerment, worthiness, expansion, and independence, regardless of your situations and circumstances.
- Achieve the "unachievable" in your mind and heart.

Coaching shows you how to:

- Rise and shine into your leadership so that you can be of the best service to yourself and others.
- Recreate and restore yourself to your better version every day, regardless of what's happened in the past. And the best

coaches know how to help you with healing the past, living more in the present, and expanding your vision to walk into a brighter future.

- Break free from the judgements, criticisms, and your opinions of self and others to live the purpose-driven life that you are called to live.

In your experience, what are some common misconceptions people have about coaching, and how do you address them to demonstrate its true value?

There are many misconceptions that people have about coaching. The first one that comes to mind is that coaching is like therapy. Therapy focuses on addressing past traumas to function better in the present, whereas coaching focuses on addressing where you want to go in the future and how to make changes in your present to get there. As mentioned previously, my perception is that the best coaches know how to help with the past, present, and future. I've found that harping on the past can sometimes cause more damage in the present, and most therapy never gets to the root causes of the problem. Therapy is very important, especially for significant past-based trauma. However, empowerment coaching (coaching of the mind and heart), can heal past trauma faster and allow you to be more present and have a "fresh start" and a new, lighter way forward.

In my coaching, I start off with a business breakthrough session. A breakthrough session releases all the mental and emotional blocks around your business and life. It's a 'spring cleaning' of the mind, heart, body, and soul. This takes care of the past traumas (including root causes) and blocks that will get in the way of you being completely successful in achieving your love and revenue goals. I find that, with this approach, the transformation of the coaching process happens faster, with more energy, and flow for your Total Exponential Acceleration (ETA). Right away, your whole mind, heart, body, and soul align to the essence of who you are. Then, every inspired action taken afterwards comes from your wisdom, which is always right. This makes the coaching process easier, and more enjoyable and enhances greater achievement for both the client and coach.

What kind of problems do you solve? Can you tell us a bit about the process that you walk people through?

We don't attract what we want as much as we attract what we are. If you have gone through significant emotional events in your past, such as being raised with trauma, abuse, and neglect, you may tend to attract a life of chaos (toxic relationships, work challenges, health issues, etc.), and this can impact business consistency, prosperity, and enjoyment. It can produce feelings of wanting to give up or that business and/or life will always be this way. This can cause relationships, connection, and communication with God, Self, and Others to suffer. There is a way to change and shift the pattern.

Big picture, I guide women bosses, who are challenged by unharmonious situations, relationships, and environments, and struggle with fear of being seen, heard, and felt, to reclaim their power, joy, and wholeness to own their Queendom! Then, they have a solid foundation to love and live the Business/Life Harmony of Their Dreams, unapologetically. We do this using a 3-step process:

1. **Lean In** - Cultivate Awareness. All change starts with awareness.
2. **Let Go** - Be the change you wish to see. This is my favorite step because most don't know how to let go, with Aloha and Forgiveness. Becoming a master of energy, mindset, and

emotions, makes this process simple, rapid, and automatic.

3. **Leap Forward** - When you become calm amid chaos (the eye of the storm), the chaos around you disappears. All that's left is unconditional love, faith, wisdom, power, and strength and it can radiate out through you to your loved ones, community, and world. Your love can heal all things.

Do you have a story about a client and how they achieved success with your coaching? Please give details.

This is best displayed with a few testimonials:

One-on-One Coaching:

"Before coming to Dr. Heather, I used to let a lot of things bother me. Now, after 6 weeks [1-hr sessions], I don't dwell on or stress about things as before. I feel more in the flow of business and life with better time management and control. I didn't think that such progress could be made so quickly. I'm now stronger and standing in my power, level-headed. Dr. Heather's coaching was a very valuable experience. I see a big difference and can truly feel the energy that I have now...not just physical, but all around." Amber A., CEO of Amber's Day Care

"After working with Dr. Heather for just 6 weeks [1-hr sessions], I was able to come off of not 1, but 3 behavioral altering medications through the guidelines of my health care provider. I had been on these medications for almost 20 years, was misdiagnosed as bipolar, and had severe anxiety. Dr. Heather taught me how to dissipate my anxiety and hear my inner voice of direction loud and clear. I'm doing better than I ever have in my entire life with communication without emotional triggers." -Nikki R., Trauma Coach of Pamper Your

Problems Co.

After this, Nikki became a certified Life Harmony Coach and NLP Master Practitioner with my company. She is now a trauma coach working with kids and young adults and does amazing things for her family and community.

Life Harmony Coach/Emotional Intelligence Expert Certification Training:

"I took Dr. Heather's class in February and implemented it in March. By April, I was hitting 10K, which is barely scratching the surface to the potential her systems provided. I am excited for the 20k or 30k months but I'm most excited that Dr. Heather's Mastery classes have given me a foundation and confidence to help anyone see their full potential while having the clarity and life harmony that they deserve." - Dr. Kelley G., Career Coach of ISO Life Coaching

Communication (Mind) Mastery / NLP Practitioner Certification Training:

"This program has been nothing short of life-affirming, providing me with the skills and tools to become aware of how I communicate with myself and others. The program has equipped me with the skills, awareness, and resilience needed to navigate life's challenges with confidence. I highly recommend this program to anyone seeking personal and professional growth, as well as those in mentorship roles who aim to help others refine their mindsets. It is a transformative experience that will undoubtedly lead to long-lasting positive change." – Sabrina T., JD, Business Coach of Impact Life Enterprises, LLC.

Did you go through the difficulties that you now help people with? Tell us about that and how it led you to become a coach.

At an early age, I went through several traumas. I was molested three times before the age of 10. I had just turned four the first time. I was not aware of these traumas or even the damage of them until my mid-30s. My grandfather, also a successful entrepreneur, was murdered when I was five. These significant emotional and physical events, unbeknownst to me, greatly impacted my health and relationships and damaged the value and worth I saw in myself. My suppressed emotions were masked by overachievement and valuing external success greater than myself. I became almost 100% for others and 0% for myself and operated this way for many years. My mind was overwhelmed, stressed (PTSD), and anxious. My heart was angry, guarded, and detached. My body was in pain, and I had no clue. I unconsciously gained weight as a form of protection. I normally experienced burnout, sickness, and overworked myself.

Relationships, especially intimate relationships, were hard for me. I would attract those who were angry, guarded, and detached. I would end up in relationships that were domestically violent, never physically, but emotionally, mentally, spiritually, financially, and relationally. I built my success and happiness in my career because that was the one area that I "control," until the work environments too became "unsafe" to stay in. So, I operated in flight and fear, especially in relationships. There was great fear of abandonment, betrayal, and mistrust of others. So many heart wounds guarded my Aloha.

The pivotal moment for me that led me to change how I do things was when I married my husband. He is a Purple Heart Marine Corps

Veteran with Post-Traumatic Stress. I became the instant mom to his son, a 1.5-year-old boy (now 10). We now have two additional girls of our own. My husband also suffered from past relationship trauma, and our marriage repeated most of our previous relationship projections. I found myself being torn down, unappreciated, belittled, devalued, and unloved. This killed my self-confidence and self-esteem in my ability to succeed as a mom, wife, and CEO.

With all the chaos in my life side, it was hard to stay confident, clear, consistent in, and passionate about myself and my business. The grief of what had happened and anxiety about what could happen created a self-imposed glass ceiling when it came to my business and what's possible for my life.

The game-changing secret I learned, through my faith and coaches, is that all my relationships are reflections of me. Even my husband's fear was being projected onto me. When I stopped listening and taking in other people's judgments and perceptions about me and paid more attention to what God says about me, I was able to fall in love with all that I am. It changed how I saw myself as well as how others saw me. I became calm, and all the chaos around me, too, became calm. With years of guiding others in their healing, I was also being healed and restored. It restored others around as well. I came from a very dark place, and now, there is so much more confidence, hope, inspiration, empowerment, abundance, prosperity, and blessings all around me 24/7. My life now just gets better and better every day. I know that if I have gone through these things and overcome them, anyone can.

If someone were fearful of coaching, what would you tell them?

There is nothing to fear but fear itself. Most people, especially those who have experienced trauma, see fear as "Forget Everything and Run." This can only take us so far. It is so much easier to run and avoid pain. If we do not heal from what hurts us or is unconsciously blocking us, we will bleed all over those who do not deserve it. We will lose out and push away the very things that God wants to bless us with. Hurt people, hurt people, and healed people, heal people. If we do not heal what has broken us, we will bleed all over people who don't deserve it. It's important to redefine fear to "Face Everything and Rise" so that you can "Feel Everything and Relax."

Coaching provides a safe, confidential, and judgment-free zone where it is safe to be you, express what is going on, feel heard and acknowledged, heal, and act on the steps that you produce for the way forward. What we resist, persists, and small problems become big mountains if we do not address them. Coaching allows you to redefine fear for yourself to easily "Face Everything and Rise" so that you can "Feel Everything and Relax." Breakthroughs and blessings happen much faster with coaching.

What would you tell someone who thinks they should be able to fix/solve this on their own?

Often, when we try to solve or fix something on our own, we start with good intentions and actions towards achievement, and then we fall off and go back into our regular patterns and behaviors. The beauty of coaching is the accountability, identifying and breaking through blocks as they arise to move forward with making permanent lasting changes on your own. Going the battle alone, you feel alone and that no one understands how you feel. Having support lets you know that you got this, and you are covered, even when it seems dim. Just reach out and try it; you will be so glad that you did!

How has being a coach and guiding others to empowerment influenced and changed your life?

In my opinion, coaching is the greatest calling that one could pursue. It leads to speaking, teaching, writing, being a show host, and so much more. Coaching really is the best form of communication. Coaching brings awareness to how to win your inner struggles and become totally successful in the way that aligns with you. Coaching is good for self, others, and the planet. Because of being a coach and having coaches myself, I am an entirely different and better person than I was.

Being a coach has transformed all areas of my life. I now see others and myself the way God does. My empathy and communication for those around me have expanded to limitless levels. I have been able to positively influence and naturally impact others around me just by my presence alone and by being the change that I wish to see in the world. My life is now stress-free and full of ease, grace, and aloha. My mind, body, and soul feel at least ten years younger than me. I am excited about all that life offers and look forward to living my elderly years.

What is the biggest takeaway about the power of coaching to remember?

Jeremiah 29:11 says, "For the plans I have for you", declares the Lord, "plans to Prosper you and not harm you, plans to give you Hope and a Future." You are the captain of your ship and the master of your fate. Your healing is in your hands. It is easy to blame others for your circumstances. I challenge you to take charge of your life and not go to battle alone. Coaching offers you the right support that will be the biggest cheerleader in your transformation to a better life. You have a calling in your life and a purpose. It is time to live it, and

I promise that your life can and will transform into all the amazement you are destined to experience. Victory is already yours if you choose to walk in it.

Are there a few steps or tips you can give someone right now to start them on their transformation?

When things are difficult or challenging, turn above and inside to wonder. Ask yourself a few questions:

- Are you living the plans God has for your life or are you living according to your plans?
- Is your will in alignment with God's will?
- Do you see yourself the way God sees you? Do you see others the way God sees them?
- Are you holding on to past hurts that are causing weight and burdens in your present?
- What are the behaviors and patterns you have that you want to change and what do you want instead?

Simply, starting with answering these questions from your heart, not the head, will start steering you in the right direction.

Do you have a gift/session that you can offer us?

Yes, I have 2 for you:

- Here's my free guide on the *7 Secrets to More Biz/Life Harmony*: www.AnotherLevelLiving.com/Harmony
- Schedule your *Complimentary Freedom Call*. In this call, I will identify your biggest unconscious Success Block and I guarantee it's not what you think it is: www.AnotherLevelLiving.com/Freedom

About the Author
Dr. Heather H. Tucker

Dr. Heather Tucker is a Business and Life Harmony Trainer. She uses unique approaches that show you how to Increase Your Confidence, Calm, and Cash Flow to bring in more clients into your business, charge what you deserve, and create more freedom in your work, relationships, and all areas of life. Her Company, Another Level Living, Inc. is a professional training company that produces deep, powerful transformations for entrepreneurs worldwide who want to overcome great challenges and stand fully in their power, unshakable, so that they can master communication and relationships in both business and life with ease and grace. After working with Dr. Heather, students find themselves working smarter, more present and in the flow, and can leap forward in their destiny and get results. Dr. Heather has certified over 400 Life coaches and 50 communication (mind) experts in her company. She is the Project Manager and Lead Author of the International Best Seller Book Series called The Power of Coaching. She's also the Host of An Online Sensation for Entrepreneurs called The Freedom Fridays Show.

Fine Tuning Your Performance

By Trish Carr

"A smart person makes a mistake, learns from it and never makes that mistake again. A wise person finds a smart person and learns how to avoid the mistake altogether."
~Roy H. Williams

Tell us about yourself, your expertise, and your coaching niche.

Trish Carr, aka, The Result Revolutionary. My expertise is in growing your business with spot-on sales communication that works. Whether it's a one-on-one conversation, a written sales page or a stage presentation, your communication makes or breaks your opportunity.

Tell us, what does coaching mean to you?

Whether it's improving your health, your wealth or your mind, coaching changes lives for the better. It is the crucial ingredient for growth. With coaching support, you get new skills, new ideas, and ways of thinking and doing that you may never have considered.

And, when you're learning something new, or changing a habit, you may think you're doing it right, but are you? How do you know? And how do you continually get better? That's where coaching comes in. You have someone who's been there, someone with the expertise to keep you moving ahead. A coach is looking over your shoulder to tweak your performance so that you achieve far more than you could on your own.

In your experience, what are some common misconceptions people have about coaching, and how do you address them to demonstrate its true value?

Many people believe that a coach is only necessary when things go wrong and need fixing. That is simply not true. Why do the greatest athletes in the world have coaches even after they've reached the pinnacle of success? Why do they keep working with coaches even after they've retired? Because coaching propels you from where you are to where you want to be—quickly. Don't wait until things fall apart to take action. Action is what gives people the lives they truly desire. They don't settle for "not good," "just OK," or "good enough." They strive to move from OK to good, or better yet, from good to GREAT. So, take that step now. Embrace the power of coaching and transform your life.

What kind of problems do you solve? Can you tell us a bit about the process that you walk people through?

I work with sales teams, business owners and individuals who want to achieve *Revolutionary Results now*. At Women's Prosperity Network, we use an innovative approach that combines proven sales strategies with the latest behavioral science. This results in a simple formula that gets past the pitfalls often associated with selling and public speaking. This proven step-by-step method shows you how to move from "Hi, nice to meet you," to "Wow, I love what you can do for me, here's my credit card!"

Do you have a story about a client and how they achieved success with your coaching? Please give details.

Yes, many. Here are a few testimonials:

- "Tripled my revenue and had my first 6-figure year! ~BJ, accountant
- "After 12 years, I finally quit my job and my business is making money consistently." ~RT Automation Expert
- "Thank you for showing me how to sell without feeling like I'm selling. LOL! I have more confidence. I actually look forward to making sales calls and my bank account is proof! ~CD Digital Marketing
- "6X'd my sales in only 90 days." ~SP, book publisher
- "Thanks for showing me a sales process that really works. Not only am I making more money, I'm doing what I love and making a difference in people's lives." ~SP, EMT Prevention Expert
- "I set a goal to earn $10K per month by the end of the year. With Trish's coaching, I hit it in only 5 months." ~SD, health coach

Did you go through the difficulties that you now help people with? Tell us about that and how it led you to become a coach.

You know, when I first started working in sales, I was absolutely terrified. I mean, I wasn't good at it at all. But here's the blessing—I was fortunate to be in a company that truly valued coaching and training. This environment allowed me to learn, tweak, learn again, and grow, all with the incredible support of mentors and coaches who genuinely wanted to see me excel. With their guidance, I gained confidence. Consistent feedback was my lifeline. I knew exactly what I did well and what I didn't because I had these amazing teachers showing me the way.

And then, something extraordinary happened. I became the #1 top seller, month after month. This success opened a new chapter in my journey—I was asked to mentor my co-workers. Eventually, I became their boss, and then their boss, and so on. My skills as a leader, trainer, and mentor blossomed, and let me tell you, it lit me up like nothing else. That's the power of growth, support, and believing in your potential. It's about embracing the journey, learning from every experience, and then sharing that light with others. That's how we all rise together.

I believe with every fiber of my being that life is a magnificent journey, a series of transformative moments that guide us ever closer to our true purpose. And for me, my path towards coaching was no exception.

One of my earliest experiences in mentoring and coaching unfolded in the heart of corporate America, within the bustling confines of a sales call center predominantly filled with women. What struck me was the sheer tenacity of these women, juggling the demands of motherhood, homemaking, and full-time work, all while striving just to keep their heads above water. But here's the thing—too often, the focus was solely on the 'how' of their jobs, neglecting the crucial 'what' and 'why.'

What drove them? What trials were they facing in their lives? Why did they find themselves in their current circumstances? And, perhaps most importantly, how did these circumstances impact their performance, their psyche, and their overall happiness? These questions ignited a spark within me, a realization that true transformation comes not just from mastering the 'how,' but from delving deep into the 'what' and 'why.'

With coaching, we didn't just enhance their performance; we ignited a revolution of empowerment. They soared to new heights, taking on greater responsibilities, more authority, and a newfound sense of autonomy. Morale in the call center soared, stress levels plummeted, and they earned more while feeling less burdened. And as a delightful bonus for the company, profits soared alongside their personal growth.

But that was just the beginning. The second defining moment came with the birth of Women's Prosperity Network, amidst the tumult of the global recession in 2008. Against all odds, my sisters (yes, blood sisters) and I embarked on a mission to create a new kind of networking—one that celebrated the spirit of 'co-opetition,' where women could come together to collaborate, expand their businesses and careers, all while staying true to themselves. From that, WPN expanded organically and naturally to include training, coaching and consulting.

So, why do coaches start their coaching business? Why did I? Because I am passionate about helping others, driven by a sense of purpose, eager to make a lasting impact, and committed to building powerful connections. It's a journey of the heart, one that calls me to step up, step out, and share my light with the world. And in doing so, I create ripples of transformation that touch countless lives. What could be better than that?

If someone were fearful of coaching, what would you tell them?

To anyone out there who's feeling a tad hesitant about working with a coach, I want you to know this: it's completely natural to have reservations about stepping into the unknown. But let me share a few words that might just ease those worries and ignite a spark of possibility within you.

First and foremost, working with a coach is not about admitting defeat or weakness. In fact, it's quite the opposite. It takes strength and courage to recognize that you want to grow, to evolve, and to reach for more in your life. A coach is simply a guide, a partner on your journey of self-discovery and transformation.

And let's talk about those nagging doubts and fears that might be holding you back. A coach is there to help you navigate through them, to shine a light on your strengths, and to empower you to overcome obstacles with grace and resilience. They create a safe space for you to explore your dreams, confront your fears, and step boldly into the life you were meant to live.

But perhaps, most importantly, working with a coach is an investment in yourself. It's a powerful declaration that you are worthy of growth, of happiness, and of living a life that truly lights you up from the inside out. And trust me when I say this—the moment you take that first step, you open the door to a world of infinite possibilities. So, to anyone who's hesitating, I encourage you to take a leap of faith. Embrace the journey, trust in the process, and know that you have everything within you to create the life of your dreams. Working with a coach might just be the catalyst you need to unlock your fullest potential and soar to new heights.

What would you tell someone who thinks they should be able to fix/solve this on their own?

You might be wondering, "Do I really need a coach? Can't I just figure things out on my own?" And you absolutely can! But here's the thing—working with a coach can *accelerate your progress in ways you never thought possible*. They're like a trusted confidant, a sounding board, and a cheerleader all rolled into one. They ask the right questions, challenge you to dig deeper, and provide invaluable insights that can propel you forward.

How has being a coach and guiding others to empowerment influenced and changed your life?

Coaching is about connection. Coaches understand the power of human connection. We know that in those one-on-one moments when we are fully present with a client, magic happens. Lives change, dreams take flight, and possibilities expand. Starting my own coaching business gave me the opportunity to build these connections on my own terms, and to cultivate relationships that are deeply meaningful and impactful. OMG, it doesn't get any better than that.

What is the biggest takeaway about the power of coaching to remember?

At its core, coaching is about empowerment. It's not about giving advice or telling someone what to do, although we do that as well. Instead, though, it's about asking the right questions, helping individuals discover their own answers, supplementing with my knowledge and expertise and encouraging them to take action. A coach is there to support, challenge, and inspire you to reach heights you might not have believed possible.

Are there a few steps or tips you can give someone right now to start them on their transformation?

You know, taking steps to effect change in your life is one of the most empowering things you can do. It's about acknowledging where you are, envisioning where you want to be, and taking actionable steps to get there. Here are some practical steps you can start with right now:

1. **Set Clear Goals**: The first step is knowing what you want to achieve. Take some time to reflect on your aspirations and write down your goals. Make them specific, measurable, attainable, relevant, and time-bound (SMART). This gives you a clear roadmap to follow.

2. **Create a Vision Board**: Visualizing your goals can be incredibly powerful. Gather images, quotes, and items that represent what you want to achieve and create a vision board. Place it somewhere you'll see every day. This constant visual reminder can keep you motivated and focused.

3. **Develop a Plan**: Break your goals into smaller, manageable steps. Create a plan that outlines what you need to do daily, weekly, and monthly to move closer to your goals. Having a detailed plan makes the process less overwhelming and more actionable.

Remember, affecting change in your life is a journey, not a destination. It's about taking consistent, intentional steps toward the life you envision. Trust in the process, believe in yourself and know that every step you take brings you closer to the change you desire. You have the power within you to create the life you want—start today and let your journey of transformation begin.

Do you have a gift/session that you can offer us?

Yes, of course! I have 2…

1. I like structure and I like formulas I can use again and again to save time. Here is the 3-step "Presentation Profitizer"™ formula for influential presentations. Equipped with this proven method, you'll close more sales in less time! https://speakingforfunandprofit.com

2. AND connect with extraordinary, heart-centered women and get your FREE membership started at: https://womensprosperitynetwork.com

About the Author
Trish Carr

Trish Carr is on a mission to show women entrepreneurs how to create messaging magic without being 'salesy.' Best-selling author, international speaker, and acclaimed sales expert. Trish combines proven communication strategies with behavioral science, resulting in a formula that gets past pitfalls associated with selling.

She is co-founder of Women's Prosperity Network, the global community for impact-driven women, dedicated to inspiring, supporting and educating women within a trusted network of professionals. Women's Prosperity Network provides online and in-person business-building and skill-building tools and trainings, inspiration and consulting programs for anyone striving to achieve their goals and live their dreams.

Unlock Your Potential

By Stephanie Richardson

"If you don't create the future you want, you endure the future you get." ~John Maxwell

Tell us about yourself, your expertise, and your coaching niche.

I am grateful you are seeking to learn more about the power of coaching. My name is Stephanie Richardson, and I am a certified leadership coach, speaker, and trainer. I provide individual coaching for CEOs, business owners, and entrepreneurs. I hold my clients accountable for reaching goals in six areas of their life, not only business goals, because each area is interconnected and affects the others. I help clients gain increased awareness and insight into their personality style and know their strengths as well as areas of opportunity for growth. With organizations, I help teams improve their communication skills among the team members and learn communication do's and do not's.

I am a Certified World Class Speaking Coach, helping professionals increase their confidence in their public speaking skills and closing ratios through a group course and individual coaching. Because of my expertise, leadership, and speaking skills, I am a keynote speaker who shares at professional conferences, association meetings, Chamber of Commerce meetings, women's organizations, and staff retreats. I also provide professional development training for organizations.

Tell us, what does coaching mean to you?

I wish more professionals were aware of how coaching can dramatically change their results and the level of satisfaction in their lives. I hope after reading this book, more professionals will be less hesitant to bet on themselves by investing in their personal growth through coaching. As a coach, I know the power of accountability through coaching, as I have invested in both individual and group coaching for myself for years, and I continue to do so. If you want to be an effective coach, you need to experience coaching for yourself.

A coach's role is to ask clients challenging questions, so they increase their awareness and personal insight. A coach is an accountability partner and catalyst for change in clients' lives. High performers always have a coach at their side to ask them the difficult questions they won't ask themselves. My goal is for my clients to feel they are successfully achieving their goals and that they are increasing their belief and confidence in themselves as they have more "wins". An effective coach's clients feel they have a safe space to be vulnerable and transparent. The coach acts as a sounding board, and encourager, and stretches clients outside of their comfort zones until the task they thought was once so daunting becomes one they handle with confidence. Then, they move on to the next task to stretch themselves yet again.

In your experience, what are some common misconceptions people have about coaching, and how do you address them to demonstrate its true value?

Many of my clients have never experienced coaching before our partnership, so they don't know what to expect, and some are nervous when they begin the coaching relationship. It's important to set expectations in the beginning about the process of the coaching relationship and what the roles are of the coach and the client. I think some clients have the misconception that a coach is going to tell them what to do, and they don't want to experience that, so they avoid coaching. I will offer suggestions after asking permission, and my role as the coach is to ask thought-provoking questions so the client independently comes to a decision.

Another misconception potential clients may have is that coaching is expensive, and they fear they won't see a return on their investment. I have some chiropractors I coach who were seeing 100 patients a month when we first started working together and now, they are seeing over 500 patients a month! Imagine how much that increased their revenue! They saw a huge return on their investment.

The best investment you can make is in yourself. Growth's highest reward is not what you get from it, but who you become because of it. The person you are when you begin coaching and the person you become in the process will be totally different.

What kind of problems do you solve? Can you tell us a bit about the process that you walk people through?

I serve as a catalyst for change in six areas of a client's life: business, personal growth, financial, spiritual, relationships, and health/fitness. Because of this focus on the six areas, clients feel more balance in their lives and report feeling more at peace. I give an initial assessment to clients to measure their level of satisfaction in each of these areas and then work with them to set goals for the year in each area. I meet with clients every two weeks in person or virtually if they live out of the area. Clients complete a coaching prep sheet before each session to share what they have accomplished in the last two weeks and identify what they want to focus on during the session. At the end of each session, we agree on what action steps the client will take for the next two weeks, so the client has a clear plan of the next steps to take.

Most clients in every industry want to increase their revenue and the number of clients they have. I have helped clients double and triple their revenue for their business and significantly increase the number of clients they have. Those who are in sales want to improve the sales process and gain confidence in how they present to potential clients. I have helped clients in sales develop a streamlined process for their presentation and helped educate clients on assumptive language to use to get more clients to take action and choose their services. One client asked me to hold her accountable to her financial goals, which included many home improvement projects, paying off debt, and graduating her college students with no debt.

Another client of mine wanted to be at the weight he was 10 years ago but he was skeptical he could reach that goal. He wanted to not get winded when he went hiking or walking with his children. We tracked his weight, what he ate, his exercise plan, worked on his positive affirmations, and he reached his goal in a few months and has maintained his goal weight for over a year. How do you think that impacted him professionally? His confidence in himself increased dramatically, and he pursued a new career path he had been wanting to pursue. Working with the whole person is motivating to me because I can see the results in clients' personal lives, not only in their business.

Do you have a story about a client and how they achieved success with your coaching? Please give details.

I have found that many physical therapists, chiropractors, counselors, and physicians are highly skilled in their craft, but they don't get exposure in their formal education on how to run their own business. I have a physical therapist I have coached for 2 1/2 years who I have helped reach personal and professional goals. With her business, we worked on marketing and how to network in the community to increase the number of clients she had. We identified where she could network and how to present her pitch to the group. We focused on having a presence on social media, and she creates videos she posts regularly as well as sending out a client newsletter. We worked on her presentation format when presenting to networking groups. We identified ways she could increase the number of clients through presentations in the community with running clubs, athletes, and referral partnerships with physicians.

She has doubled the number of clients she has and has pursued additional streams of revenue within her business. She has achieved personal growth through additional training and certifications. She has developed a morning routine of journaling and has a consistent exercise regimen, including participating in various marathons. Personally, she has set aside weekend getaway trips with her husband and date nights, as well as trips with extended family. She said that before we started working together, she set some goals but felt she allowed herself to ignore some areas of her life. She feels coaching has helped her create a better version of herself and create her life on purpose.

Did you go through the difficulties that you now help people with? Tell us about that and how it led you to become a coach.

I have been a single mom for most of my daughter's life. It has been challenging raising a child on my own. When you are a single parent, you don't have the support from a spouse to help with caring for your child daily, making decisions about your child's education path, making financial decisions, or decisions about caring for your home. Of course, you can consult with family and friends, but you make the final decision yourself. I felt the weight of those responsibilities.

I can relate to clients who are single parents, those who have a spouse who travels so frequently that it feels like they are a single parent, as well as those who are married and don't have appropriate support from their spouse. Learning how to effectively balance family time and work is an area I have had success managing. Many of my clients struggle with balance, and I feel I can help them feel more at peace with balance. I have been an entrepreneur for 27 years. I took the leap and quit my corporate job and changed careers to direct sales because I saw a way to be able to raise my daughter without putting her in daycare.

When clients have a dream to leave the corporate world and start their own business, I can relate to the challenges and mountain-top experiences that come with being an entrepreneur because I have successfully started and run two businesses of my own. I have also experienced financial challenges. When I started my direct sales business, I had several thousands of dollars in credit card debt, which I paid off in the first year of my direct sales business. I can relate to clients who have financial challenges and can share what strategies I used to get out of debt, stay out of debt, and pay cash for purchases. I think it's important as a coach to be vulnerable and share the challenges you have experienced to build an authentic relationship with your clients.

It's important to pay attention to doors that open in your life and walk through them with the confidence that it is your path outlined for you to take. When I felt the nudge to quit my corporate job and stay home with my daughter, I cried and prayed an entire weekend and had peace with my decision to put her as a priority, although it was a financial risk to leave a steady income and pursue a career that was 100% commission. When clients experience fear or hesitation with starting a business or taking a financial risk, I can easily relate to that fear of the unknown.

There was a pivotal moment in my life that inspired me to pursue coaching. I was attending a women's networking group as a representative of my direct sales business, and a woman who coached other women coaches asked me why I had not pursued a coaching business. She told me that my background as a therapist made me different from other coaches, and that I had years of experience of coaching and developing others in the direct sales industry that would transfer. That was the first nudge I received.

If someone were fearful of coaching, what would you tell them?

I have found that some clients are fearful because they have never been in a coaching relationship before and don't know what to expect. Some clients are hesitant to invest in themselves financially. Some clients have verbalized to me that they fear they won't follow through on the commitment it takes to see results. Coaching is a two-way relationship, and both the client and the coach need to be treated with respect. For anyone who is hesitant to engage in coaching, I would suggest a trial period of three months. I ask for that commitment from my clients, and if they want to discontinue coaching after those three months or decrease the frequency, that is agreeable.

What would you tell someone who thinks they should be able to fix/solve this on their own?

High performers always have a coach by their side to ask them the difficult questions they won't ask themselves. Why is it important to have an accountability partner? Being involved in coaching entrepreneurs for 27 years, I have found there is a small percentage of people who are self-accountable and self-motivated. Most people tend to tell themselves that they will take action tomorrow or next week and procrastinate. Anything worth having is going to be tough, and navigating the struggle of your challenges is necessary with an accountability partner.

Human beings are tribal by nature and need community, and a coach provides a sense of community and someone who is invested in seeing you transform yourself. An accountability partner gives you the structure you need to grow. When you are investing in coaching, you are investing in your future self, in who you will become through the process. Why does that matter? Because you will be stretched outside of your comfort zone, so you grow and feel more and more unstoppable. The more "wins" you have, the more your confidence increases in yourself. You will be held accountable for transforming yourself into the person you want to become. Bet on yourself or encourage someone you know to bet on himself or herself to start your coaching journey.

How has being a coach and guiding others to empowerment influenced and changed your life?

The transformation you see in your clients is so exciting to watch! It is extremely rewarding to feel, in some small way, you have contributed as a coach to the change you see in clients, to the insight and self-awareness they have gained, seeing how they have stretched themselves out of their comfort zone, and how that contributed to an increase in their confidence.

Holding others accountable to their goals makes me as a coach more self-aware in reaching my own goals. I get to practice in my own life what I am sharing with my clients. Therefore, I'm consistently engaging in additional training and attending professional development conferences. I have my own coach to hold me accountable for my goals. I get to have a consistent reminder of what it is like to be in the client role and to know the emotions, struggles, and rewards they experience. This helps me continue to strengthen my emotional relationship with clients and increase my empathy level.

What is the biggest takeaway about the power of coaching to remember?

The biggest takeaway about the power of coaching to remember is that you can create your life on purpose and become the best version of yourself with the guidance, support, and thought-provoking questions provided by your coach. A coach is not emotionally connected to the outcomes of your life and business and therefore helps guide your decisions with an outside and unbiased perspective that can be helpful and insightful for the client.

Your success in life is going to be the result of your own personal growth, and coaching is an empowering method to grow yourself. Personal growth doesn't happen on its own. When you grow yourself, you grow your business and become a new person through the process.

Are there a few steps or tips you can give someone right now to start them on their transformation?

It's important to assess where you are currently, and then determine where you want to be.

1. Look at your current level of satisfaction in six areas of your life, including business, health/fitness, spiritual, financial, personal growth, and relationships. Rate your level of satisfaction on a scale of 1 to 10, with 10 being a high level of satisfaction.
2. Determine what are some goals that you want to accomplish in each of those 6 areas and write them down in a journal or save them in your notes on your phone.
3. Identify the next best step you are willing to take in each area to move you closer to achieving your goals.
4. Determine who will be your accountability partner to help you stay on track. I would be honored to be your partner!

Do you have a gift/session that you can offer us?

I provide a free weekly video newsletter that is a 1-2 minute video with a motivational and inspirational topic that will increase your growth and self-awareness. You can also schedule your complimentary consultation with me. Simply, go to my website: www.StephanieRichardsonUYP.com

About the Author
Stephanie Richardson

Stephanie Richardson's goal is to add value to your life so you walk away with specific action steps you can take to empower yourself, improve your business results, and help you move closer to where you want to be. Stephanie has an M.S. in psychology. Stephanie utilizes her skills as a retired Licensed Professional Counselor with over 10 years of experience in the counseling field. She shares with her clients the lessons she has learned through 27 years of training, coaching, and leading a multi-million dollar-a-year direct sales organization of almost 1600 members, with significant results in the areas of promoting and developing 80 leaders across the nation. Stephanie is a Certified World Class Speaking Coach and teaches others how to improve their confidence in their speaking skills and closing ratios. She helps individuals, couples, teens, and organizations understand themselves more deeply and improve communication with others as a DISC Consultant. She is a Maxwell Leadership Team certified trainer, keynote speaker, and business/life coach, being a catalyst for change in her coaching clients' lives and providing accountability toward taking the steps needed to achieve their vision.

Creating Magical Steps

By Sheryl Bernstein

"A dream is a wish your heart makes." – Jiminy Cricket

Tell us about yourself, your expertise, and your coaching niche.

I'm Sheryl Bernstein, The Creative Muse. I'm a Visibility Coach and Creative Producer & Director. I help coaches and entrepreneurs create the pieces that support their business, increase their visibility, add ease to their work, and connection to their clients and future clients. Clarity and creating.

Tell us, what does coaching mean to you?

Coaching, to me, means helping someone see the possibilities that I see for them, that they cannot yet see themselves. And to bring those possibilities to life. Specifically in my work, coaching means:

To show the way to create the things they don't know how to create and teach them how to do it themselves, so they're free to take action, say yes to be seen opportunities, and put things out there anytime they wish.

1. To bring ease and joy into the 'creating business' process.
2. Provide emotional, strategic, and creative support.
3. To help my clients know (and really feel) they are not alone. They do not need to take on growing and running their business all by themselves, which can be a very lonely place to be. With my kind of coach, they have a partner, a teacher, a team, a cheerleader, and a 'Mom'.

4. To pass on my experience and knowledge to shorten the learning curve.
5. To help my clients feel well taken care of. They matter, and they have someone who wants their success as much as they do. They have a partner in this.

I can see the future version of them…because I know what can be, and how to make it happen. It's a version of them that they may not be able to envision yet themselves. It's not in focus for them…it's blurry…not filled in. Only because they don't know what is possible. Or, they may not believe it. But because I can see it…and I believe it for them…I can mentor and guide them into it.

In your experience, what are some common misconceptions people have about coaching, and how do you address them to demonstrate its true value?

Some may think there needs to be something 'wrong' with them to have a coach. But in my opinion, it's to help someone get to their goal faster. Guided by someone who knows the right path to take…knows where the pitfalls are, knows what's needed and what's a time waster…and can help speed up results. Often, a client may think they need to do a certain action, training, or thing to get the results they think they want…but a coach can see if they even have the right result in mind. I give every client the White Glove treatment… they have my attention and my caring. My coaching is not a one-size-fits-all. And my clients can feel that.

What kind of problems do you solve? Can you tell us a bit about the process that you walk people through?

I do a variety of things: help coaches and entrepreneurs set up systems, and learn how to use them (email systems, payment pages, schedulers, landing pages, videos, workshops...all sorts of behind-the-scenes systems & set up that help their business run smoothly, automated. I also direct them on video and help them look and sound their best. There's also the mindset piece. There can be a lot of feelings that come up when building a business...and being seen. I help untangle all kinds of things, from tech to how to handle a coaching problem. And because I have the experience of doing all the things...I can guide them through the quickest, simplest way to get things done, avoiding mistakes and problems. I know where the problems could pop up, and how to avoid them.

Do you have a story about a client and how they achieved success with your coaching? Please give details.

I know that when a coach or entrepreneur just has ideas in their head or notes on paper, they sometimes don't feel as if they have a 'real' business. When we finish creating the visual pieces for them, and they can SEE their name, brand, opt-in forms, freebies, and emails ready to roll, my clients say, 'Wow, NOW I feel like I have a business!' Then they're excited to take action, making offers, holding workshops & webinars, being in giveaways and summits, being seen, and building their community. They have the pieces ready to make that happen and aren't alone in the process. They have their Creative Partner. And so much more can happen on a personal level. My belief in them increases their belief in themselves. One client wrote to me: "Sheryl, Thank you, from my heart. You've been helping me get back to myself inside."

Did you go through the difficulties that you now help people with? Tell us about that and how it led you to become a coach.

When I first studied to become a Coach and got certified... (I was first a Coach in the Law of Attraction) I learned WHAT to do to be a coach...but I didn't know how to do it. How did lead magnets get created? How did they get attached to an email? How did other people send those emails? And it wasn't just from a regular email account...it was fancier. How do you do that? How did everything work so you could just click on a button and get taken to the next page, or step, or sign-up page? And how did they make those pages that told about their products and services and opt-ins for workshops, and classes, and purchases...how do they do all that?

I did not know. And I wanted to know. But I had no clue how to even start or where to find help......so I felt stuck, unable to move forward in the way I wanted. I didn't know how to find someone who could help me. And I didn't have a ton of money to throw around! I was lost. Also, back then, I was a bit intimidated by the tech that seemed to be a part of everything. (By the way, I did NOT grow up with computers! Or cell phones. Or any of the technology we have now). The tech was overwhelming and new to me. But I did find someone who showed me and taught me how, in a way I could grasp. And then, it was suggested to me that I combine what I did in the past (my background in Show Biz, performing, producing & directing) with my Law of Attraction Coaching and my new knowledge of the 'how to' for creating online business pieces. So, I blended all the parts together to create the coaching model I do now; Guiding, teaching and creating for coaches & entrepreneurs to help get their businesses created and set up. And, my specialty...patience, kindness and going at the pace that my client learns best at, especially good for clients who may feel a bit lost when it comes to tech. And we do it all with fun and ease. As one client said to me "Sheryl, you make simplicity out of the complicated!" Clarity, Creation, Visibility, Upliftment and Growth.

Looking for the Magical Stepping Stone:

Before coaching, I had a very busy, full career in show biz...writing, producing, voicing radio & TV commercials, parts on TV and film, hosted a fab radio show in L.A. Busy with auditions & bookings, making appearances. It was a Golden Time for me. But after about 20 years in the biz...things began to change. There was more 'at home' auditioning. More non-union work and people doing it. The magical clique of voiceover that I was a part of began to disappear. Producers I worked with moved on. The style of voice they were looking for changed (as it often does). And my work became less and less. I didn't like that my income changed...but an even bigger disappointment was the not being busy, not being in demand, not having the fun of going to the big fancy studios with the valet parking and the kitchens stocked with all kinds of goodies for us voiceover actors. We were treated like movie stars. I still had bookings, but it wasn't like the booming, abundant gig-to-gig constantly-booked career that I had experienced for almost 2 decades. And it was happening for a lot of us. Things change. So, when all that high-level action began to dwindle and go away...I did not like it. I felt unwanted. Not valued anymore. My talents and creativity were not being utilized. It was like the biz was telling me I was done. But I was NOT done. Not done working, not done contributing my talents and abilities, not done being part of the creative process that making commercials was. Not done feeling the buzz when I'd get a call from my agent, "Hey you booked such and such a spot". Not done being in the exciting whirl and special clique that my showbiz /advertising

/voiceover world was. But I didn't know what I was going to do next. What could I do? What did I want to do?

Where was my magical stepping stone? It always lit up for me in the past. Showing me the direction. Where was it now? Why wasn't anything showing me the way? Giving me a hint...a sign...of what might be next for me. My special thing.

Then one day, I got an email from a woman named Christy Whitman. Didn't know it then, but she's one of the Premier Coaches and Teachers of the Law of Attraction. And this was one of her lead magnets. (Also didn't know anything about those back then.) She offered a course on '7 Laws of the Universe.' I'd never heard of that before....sounded so interesting. So I clicked the button, put in my name and email, and over the next few weeks received the 7 lessons. Around email 6, Christy offered some free Law of Attraction coaching. She had a Coaching Academy and her coaches needed practice. I had never heard of coaching (Coaching? What's that??). But again, I was intrigued, so I said yes, I'd like the 3 sessions. We met on the phone. (No zoom yet). We talked, she asked questions, helped me think things through, and entertained new ideas. I really don't remember what we talked about exactly, but I do remember this: right after our session, I said to myself "THAT!! THAT is what I want to do now. I want to help others feel just like she made me feel." Like anything was possible. I was filled with joy, and light...felt energized, weightless and unlimited. "This is my next. I want to be a Coach!" So I became a Certified Coach in the Law of Attraction. And after that learned how to be an entrepreneur. I combined my background in showbiz, with my Law of Attraction Coaching, and now help coaches and entrepreneurs build their businesses and create the things that will help them show up, be seen and known.

If someone were fearful of coaching, what would you tell them?

I would say try out 1 session. Let your coach know that you're fearful. A good coach will totally understand, and be compassionate about it. Most coaches would be happy to let you have a 1 or 2-session paid trial.

And listen to your gut, your intuition. There'll be a coach that's just right for you. It'll just feel right. It's a relationship, some will fit you, some won't. It's a mix of the energy, voice, spirit, tempo, and the way they work, listen and speak. How do you feel before, during and after a session? You'll know when it feels right. You can meet a lot of coaches by having their free Discovery or Intro calls. Take advantage of those. And don't be pressured to jump into anything. You get to take your time to make a choice, you get to think about it. I do not believe that anyone should be pressured into coaching.

What would you tell someone who thinks they should be able to fix/solve this on their own?

Well, you might be able to fix it on your own. But having a coach, the right coach, can move you through faster. Ask yourself: "Can I really fix this on my own?" And how long have you been trying? What gets in the way of solving it?" Also ask this: What if you had someone you really liked, and they helped you solve your problem? And you felt better and better after every session, and could see real progress? And didn't feel alone in this anymore, and felt like someone's in your corner, who wants for you what you want for yourself?" Because that's what coaching can be.

How has being a coach and guiding others to empowerment influenced and changed your life?

I love my clients. I love teaching and showing them how to get the results they want. I love that they feel empowered and able to take action, and that I'm their guide. I know what I do works. All that has given me even greater self-confidence, belief in what I do, and power to take MY big steps forward. Saying yes to more. Trusting my own internal guide, higher self, intuition.

What is the biggest takeaway about the power of coaching to remember?

With the right coach, your possibilities are greater than you can imagine from where you are right now. Through the guidance of a coach with the knowledge, experience, compassion, kindness, understanding, rhythm, spirit and energy that fits you, what you seek can be yours.

Are there a few steps or tips you can give someone right now to start them on their transformation?

If you're building a coaching business I recommend getting clear on a few things:

1. Who is your ideal client? Not just a demographic, or what their problem is. Yes, those are important. But I'm talking about, who do you want to work with? How do they show up? What's their personality like? Are they on time? Can they pay? Do they do the work? Do they WANT results? Do you have fun together? And if those particular things don't matter to you... what are the qualities you would love them to have?

2. Build an email list. If you don't have it already, get yourself

an email system. Create a freebie. But make sure that freebie is calling in the people you want to work with! What is their problem at the point when YOU want to be working with them?

3. Know where you're leading your clients to. Is it a 1:1 coaching program? Group program? What is the thing you're going to be offering? And what are the results of that thing? It's important to know what you'll be offering, then everything you do and create can lead up to it.

Do you have a gift/session that you can offer us?

When you're on video, and your clients and future clients can see you, hear you, and feel you...they can really 'get' you. Your voice, rhythm, spirit...and they'll feel that much closer to you. A relationship can grow. My gift is "10 Things to Know Before You Video, to save time, help you shine, and look like a pro!" A pdf guide plus easy, fun videos to walk you through. Things I've learned from experience and I'm sharing with you so you can be ready and set when you go on camera and feel great about it. Here's where to get your free gift:

https://www.sherylbernstein.com/starlight

About the Author
Sheryl Bernstein

Sheryl Bernstein is The Creative Muse & Visibility Coach. With a background in Show Biz, performing, producing, directing, and art, plus a Law of Attraction Certified Coach, she loves to teach and guide coaches and entrepreneurs to create the pieces of their business, making sure their essence and uniqueness shine through all. With patience and intuitive clarity, she helps coaches in all areas of 'being seen' and to genuinely connect with their clients. Meeting you where you are on your business path, she can take you from vision to implementation, helping create videos, freebies, emails, writing, opt-ins, and all the visual & creative pieces that help create your business. And the mindset uplifts to empower your confidence. One of her clients said, "Sheryl, you make simplicity out of complexity." Sheryl lives in Los Angeles and loves trees, gardens, animals, and tranquility. Inspired by Nature. Powered by Light.

Rocks in the River

By Lisa Birnesser

"Courage starts by showing up and letting ourselves be seen" ~Brene Brown

Tell us about yourself, your expertise, and your coaching niche.

I am Lisa Birnesser, and I am an Empowerment Coach for Women Entrepreneurs and Business Owners. I show High-Achieving Women how to go from Overwhelmed to Empowered and Take Control of Their Schedule so that they can step into their freedom.

Tell us, what does coaching mean to you?

Coaching is synonymous with freedom. It's about liberating yourself from self-doubt and confusion to find clarity and truth. Coaching is designed to support you in your journey from where you are to where you want to be, providing personalized tools to reveal your path. It provides a safe space for self-exploration, allowing you to see your situation with fresh eyes and discover your authentic self. This process empowers you to craft unique perspectives and solutions.

Imagine having a trusted partner who sees your potential even when you don't. That's a powerful thing and what coaching offers. It's about harnessing your strengths and aligning them with your goals. Coaching isn't about fixing you; it's about revealing your true potential and helping you rise.

Each coaching session is progress toward building a solid

foundation of resilience and self-belief. With your coach by your side, you'll find the courage to take bold steps and the wisdom to navigate challenges gracefully.

In your experience, what are some common misconceptions people have about coaching, and how do you address them to demonstrate its true value?

Many people have misconceptions about coaching, which can create hesitancy and confusion about what coaching truly offers. It's important to clarify these misunderstandings and highlight the unique value of coaching.

First, coaching is not about fixing you; it's about empowering you. You are not broken. Coaching focuses on forward movement and personal growth. I address these misconceptions by showing that coaching is a partnership where you set the agenda, and together, we uncover your potential and chart a course to achieve your goals.

Another common misconception is that a coach simply tells you what to do. Coaching is a collaborative partnership. It's not about giving advice or dictating actions; it's about empowering you to find solutions. A coach asks powerful questions that help you gain insights, clarify your values, and identify your path forward. You are the expert on your life, and coaching is designed to help you tap into your inner wisdom and resources.

The most successful experiences I have had with coaches were when I could explore without judgment and those who asked powerful, insightful questions. This allowed me to listen deeply and intuitively to unearth my true self and perspective. I co-create this same space for clients within my sessions. In essence, coaching is a powerful tool for personal and professional growth. It's about unlocking your potential, overcoming obstacles, and achieving your goals with a trusted partner.

What kind of problems do you solve? Can you tell us a bit about the process that you walk people through?

As a stress mastery coach, I help women navigate stress, set boundaries, and step into their power. My process begins with a 90-minute jumpstart call, where we dig deep into a stress mastery questionnaire to pinpoint your top stressors. We then conduct a strengths assessment to identify your top five strengths and explore how to leverage them in tough situations. Additionally, we clarify your values to ensure your beliefs align with your actions, and I provide resilience tools and stress relief strategies to help you manage stress effectively. I offer several packages to cater to your individual situation.

Do you have a story about a client and how they achieved success with your coaching? Please give details.

One of my clients was overwhelmed with stress, both at work and at home. She began to have difficulties focusing and completing her projects for clients. Through our coaching sessions, we focused on stress management and resilience strategies. Over time, she transformed her stress symptoms. She could complete her projects on time and focus on what mattered most. She regained control over her life, managed her stress more effectively, and felt empowered and at peace. Seeing her transformation from a state of overwhelming to a place of empowerment and calm was a testament to the profound impact of coaching. Her success story is a powerful reminder of what's possible with the power of coaching.

Did you go through the difficulties that you now help people with? Tell us about that and how it led you to become a coach.

Absolutely. My journey into stress management coaching began in 2010 when I saw how stress affected my massage clients. There came a point where my growth and expansion of consciousness were vital to my health, business, and well-being.

During COVID-19, I faced significant stress myself, leading to depression and weight gain. Realizing the impact of my unhealthy beliefs and actions, I embarked on a health journey on May 2, 2022. I lost 110 pounds and shed toxic self-beliefs. This transformation inspired me to develop a new coaching program, blending innovative techniques with solid assessments to help others discover their true selves.

The pivotal moment for me was recognizing the profound impact of stress on my life during the pandemic. Overcoming my inner critic and failure mindset transformed my approach to coaching. Facing my struggles head-on gave me valuable insights and a compassionate, empowering approach to help others navigate similar challenges. This experience solidified my belief in resilience and self-compassion, now at the core of my coaching practice.

If someone were fearful of coaching, what would you tell them?

I would share my own experiences and encourage them to set up a time to talk. We can discuss their fears and clarify the coaching process in a safe, supportive environment. It's about creating a space where they feel heard and empowered to explore new possibilities without judgment. Coaching is a journey of growth and self-discovery, and feeling apprehensive is normal. By addressing their concerns openly, we can demystify the process and show how coaching can be a powerful tool for transformation. I'd explain that coaching is about unlocking potential, not fixing problems. It provides guidance, support, and a fresh perspective, helping them navigate challenges and achieve their goals. With the right coach, they can turn fear into growth.

What would you tell someone who thinks they should be able to fix/solve this on their own?

I would ask how long they've dealt with the issue and what steps they've taken. Often, people struggle alone for years without making progress. I'd emphasize that seeking support isn't a sign of weakness but strength and wisdom. Coaching provides new perspectives and strategies you might not see on your own. It's about having a partner who believes in your potential and helps you unlock it. We can create a plan tailored to your needs and goals by working together. Remember, even the most successful individuals seek guidance and support. With the right coach, you can break through barriers, accelerate your progress, and achieve more than you ever thought possible.

How has being a coach and guiding others to empowerment influenced and changed your life?

Being a coach and guiding others to empowerment has profoundly enriched my life. Seeing women step into their power and transform their lives fills my heart with immense joy and fulfillment. It reaffirms my belief in the strength and resilience inherent in everyone. Each client's success story inspires me to continue growing and evolving. Coaching has deepened my empathy, sharpened my listening skills, and strengthened my commitment to personal growth. It's a reciprocal journey where I learn as much from my clients as they do from me. The transformations I witness motivate me to keep pushing boundaries and exploring new ways to support and uplift others. This work has shown me the incredible impact of guidance, support, and unwavering belief in one's potential.

What is the biggest takeaway about the power of coaching to remember?

The biggest takeaway about the power of coaching is its ability to unlock untapped potential and drive profound personal growth. Coaching is not just about setting and achieving goals; it's about transforming your mindset and expanding your horizons. It empowers you to break through self-imposed limitations and discover new possibilities. Through coaching, you learn to harness your strengths, embrace challenges, and turn obstacles into opportunities. It's about building resilience, gaining clarity, and taking decisive action towards your dreams. The real power of coaching lies in its ability to help you become the best version of yourself, living authentically and purposefully. It's a journey of self-discovery that equips you with the tools and confidence to thrive in every aspect of your life.

Are there a few steps or tips you can give someone right now to start them on their transformation?

Absolutely. Here are a few steps to kickstart your transformation journey.

1. First, dedicate time just for yourself. Create a quiet, distraction-free zone where you can reflect and plan.
2. Next, identify what you truly want to achieve. Write down your goals and visualize your desired outcomes. Practice self-

compassion by being kind to yourself, acknowledging your progress, and forgiving yourself for any setbacks. Don't be afraid to seek support from a coach, mentor, or supportive friend. Having someone to guide and encourage you can make a huge difference.

3. Finally, take action by starting with small, manageable steps. Consistent action, no matter how small, will build momentum and lead to significant changes over time.

Do you have a gift/session that you can offer us?

Yes, I have 2 for you! Access your free gift called, "Quiet Your Inner Judge: 3 Keys to Self-Compassion for Women Entrepreneurs" here: www.UnlockYourInnerPotential.com/self-compassion

Additionally, schedule your complimentary session to explore your goals and challenges in a safe and supportive environment on my website here: www.UnlockYourInnerPotential.com

About the Author
Lisa Birnesser

Lisa Birnesser is an Empowerment Coach for women entrepreneurs. She shows High-Achieving Women how to Go from Overwhelmed to Empowered and Take Control of Their Schedules. Lisa stands out from others with her diverse background in coaching, operating her own business, and her innate creativity and intuition. With a Bachelor of Science in Occupational Therapy and a background in massage therapy, Lisa brings a holistic approach to her coaching practice. She is also certified in positive psychology coaching. Lisa's empathic and understanding nature empowers her clients to overcome challenges and achieve their desired outcomes. Lisa helps her clients find more time, regain their power, and create lasting life transformations through her unique blend of stress mastery techniques, resilience, meditation, and mindfulness practices.

Guiding Leaders

By Joann Bellenkes

"The greatest good you can do for another Is not just sharing your riches, but to reveal to them their own."
~Benjamin Disraeli

Tell us about yourself, your expertise, and your coaching niche.

My name is Joann Bellenkes, and I am the Founder of Sidecar Coaching. I am an Executive and Leadership coach. Having spent more than 25 years in the corporate world as both a director as well as C-Level leader, I focus my coaching on both emerging leaders, as well as incumbent leaders. I have spent the past 18 months working with Women in leadership, helping them overcome lack of confidence, perfectionism, and impostor syndrome to become confident and impactful leaders.

Tell us, what does coaching mean to you?

Coaching allows me the opportunity to really connect with individuals who, for a time, are seeking answers, clarity, or need to find a way to become unstuck due to overwhelm or fear. The fact that someone is vulnerable and open to, not only face things they may not always want to see, but also allow me to be on that journey with them, is something that never ceases to humble me. The joy I feel when my clients experience their "light bulb" moments, experience wins, or the pride they take when they see they are making strides towards their goals, is quite special. It never gets old for me, as each client has their own journey, their unique challenges, and the path they take is always new and different. I never take it for granted.

To be a part of their journey, to partner with someone when they need a boost over the wall, a hand to pull them out of the quicksand, a partner to navigate the obstacles in life or career, and to run alongside them as they cross the finish line. It is truly an honor for me.

In your experience, what are some common misconceptions people have about coaching, and how do you address them to demonstrate its true value?

There are quite a few misconceptions that people have about coaching. Some believe that a coach is going to tell them what to do to reach their goals or overcome a challenge. A coach does not tell a client what they should/should not do. A coach does not give advice or mentor. A coach is not a therapist.

Another misconception is that the coach has all the answers and will provide them. As a coach, it is not my role to provide answers but to facilitate them in discovering their own solutions and action steps. An individual is more likely to follow through with their strategies when they are the ones to determine them, rather than someone else telling them what to do.

One final misconception, though there are more, is that coaching will have immediate results. I explain to my clients at the outset, that while there may be some coaching effects that they may experience immediately, when it comes to lasting change, that requires time and effort. Coaching is about growth and discovery, and that is not something that can be rushed. I am sure to set realistic expectations and we discuss the coaching process, so they understand what is involved.

What kind of problems do you solve? Can you tell us a bit about the process that you walk people through?

In my practice, I found that many of the women in leadership, despite their success and achievements, have a common thread of several challenges: Overthinking, second-guessing themselves, feeling that they must be perfect to be respected, feeling invisible, especially to those who are senior in leadership. These are very prevalent among accomplished women. While I work with each client in a way that is designed for them specifically, I created a signature system that I use with my clients. It is the DRIVE method.

- **D**iscovery- We begin with an in-depth discovery session to understand the leader's background, challenges, aspirations, and specific areas that may be hindering their leadership potential.
- **R**eset- We focus on challenging and reframing limiting beliefs that contribute to negative self-talk, lack of confidence and overthinking. We work to replace negative thought patterns like, "I can't", with empowering beliefs like "How can I", thus fostering a more positive and resilient mindset.
- **I**mprove- We explore the leader's authentic self, helping them uncover their unique strengths, values, and leadership styles. We also identify any gaps that may need to be filled.
- **V**oice- For those who feel they have lost their voice, we delve into effective communication strategies, helping leaders express themselves confidently and with clarity.
- **E**mpower- The leaders elevate their self-confidence, trust

their instincts, recognize their worth, and embrace their resilience. They then are more empowered leaders, who are strong, confident, and ready to stand out in their leadership roles authentically and with impact.

I am able to coach people in leadership because not only did I hold leadership roles, but throughout my career, I made it a point to learn about the skills and fundamentals of leadership, communication, empathy, strategy, ethics, and have worked with others who are aspiring or already in those roles, to assist them in understanding what it means to be an impactful and respected leader, along with the many challenges that come with that great responsibility.

Do you have a story about a client and how they achieved success with your coaching? Please give details.

I have a client who is a Director at a well-known high-end luxury brand. When she came to me, though she had achieved much in her role, she said she felt invisible to her senior leaders, spent a lot of her time rehashing meetings and presentations in her head, wishing she had said things differently, and beating herself up for things she wished she had done "better". She had very low self-confidence and belief in her abilities.

I worked with her using different modalities, but her real transformation began when we talked. I come from a place of curiosity, and when she would tell me of the many programs and policies she developed and implemented, she could hear herself, as she was recounting these success stories, almost as an outside party. She realized, as she was describing these accomplishments to me, that she indeed, had accomplished a lot, was not only successful but an integral part of her organization's growth.

This was the foundation of our working together, and the beginning of many new insights into the possibilities she has before her, building her belief and confidence in herself. We include role-playing as part of our sessions, so she has a strategy and plan when she has to navigate either a new situation or one that she is not comfortable with. She has grown tremendously and is much happier and confident in her role as a leader. She is currently not only flourishing in her role, she's also awaiting a promotion which will happen in the upcoming months.

Did you go through the difficulties that you now help people with? Tell us about that and how it led you to become a coach.

My journey to becoming a coach was born out of the challenges I faced as an executive. Navigating my own struggles, I found myself in a work environment that eventually took a toll on my health. As an executive leading a team, I put in 50-60-hour weeks, constantly striving for excellence. After years of this intense workload, my team and department were running smoothly, and I was ready for a new challenge.

My manager presented me with an incredible opportunity, but it came with a catch: I had to take on this new role in addition to my already demanding responsibilities. Not wanting to appear incapable or uncooperative, I accepted the challenge. With minimal support, I spent nearly two years working.

7 days a week, 15 hours a day. My sleep suffered, my nerves were frayed, and I started experiencing memory lapses. Fearing early onset Alzheimer's, I consulted a neurologist, only to find my brain and memory were functioning well. My next stop was my physician, whom I had never met before because I rarely visited doctors. Her

immediate reaction was one of shock—she told me, "You look scary," and took me off work that very day.

With a little distance from my job, I realized that my lack of boundaries, difficulty saying "no," perfectionism and a touch of impostor syndrome had all contributed to my health crisis. A close friend suggested I explore coaching, saying that it was something I had been doing informally throughout my career. Curious, I researched accredited coaching schools and enrolled within days. Over the next 16 months, I attended classes four nights a week, coached clients pro bono, took numerous tests, and received mentoring from a Professional Certified Coach (PCC). Eventually, I earned my coaching credentials and currently hold three certifications: Certified Executive Coach (CEC), Certified Organizational Development Coach (CODC), and Certified Life Coach (CLC)

My experience as an executive, and the challenges I overcame, enabled me to coach others in leadership effectively. I understand their struggles because I've been in their shoes. I've walked their path and can guide them with the knowledge and insight gained from being a few steps ahead.

If someone were fearful of coaching, what would you tell them?

People are afraid of the unknown, that is natural. Some may be fearful of "uncovering" things they may not want to know. Coaching is not therapy, though. We are not looking back at their past. Some of the fear may also come from feeling vulnerable in revealing their thoughts and feelings to a stranger.

A good coach comes from a place of no judgement. Your discussions are completely confidential and your coach collaborates with you to support your goals. A good coach is there to guide, listen and help navigate their client's challenges. While taking that first step might be scary, the results of working with a great coach can be life-changing, and lead to profound personal and professional transformation.

What would you tell someone who thinks they should be able to fix/solve this on their own?

Even the most accomplished individuals, athletes, politicians, and leaders, have benefitted from a coach at some point to provide external support and perspective. Many times, when you are deeply involved in a situation, it is hard to "see the forest for the trees". It is not always easy to see all angles of a situation. A coach can provide an objective, unbiased perspective that can help identify blind spots and ways to overcome the obstacles. Working with a coach can often accelerate the process and development that is at times necessary to overcome challenges. Of course, there is nothing like the support and confidence a coach can provide when you have an ally who believes in you, helps motivate you, and helps boost your confidence.

How has being a coach and guiding others to empowerment influenced and changed your life?

I am humbled and honored each time a client chooses to work with me. It is a responsibility I do not take lightly or for granted. To be a part of someone's journey and transformation never loses its magic. When a client experiences an "a ha" moment or uncovers an insight that shifts their perspectives on themselves, their work, and their life, it is truly beautiful and inspiring.

Clients are never "broken" or "damaged". They truly have the answers within, but sometimes need a coach to act as a mirror and a guide to help them see what they cannot at that moment in time. Witnessing these discoveries is always special for both the client and for me. While it took me many years to discover coaching, in its true form, it is the one thing I know in my heart, without a doubt, that I love, and passionate about, and most importantly, was born to do. I look at my years of struggle as a blessing, because it led me to the career that has changed my life.

What is the biggest takeaway about the power of coaching to remember?

Where to begin? Without sounding trite, coaching can be life-changing. It transforms the way individuals perceive their potential. It is more than achieving goals, it allows you to have a deeper understanding of yourself, fosters self-awareness and hopefully cultivates a growth and resilience mindset. I have said this earlier, but clients are never broken when it comes to coaching. Once they are in the coaching process, they find that the answers and solutions they have been looking for many times are already within them.

Coaching is the tool that allows them to make that discovery. As a coach, it is incredible to experience when someone realizes they can navigate challenges they once saw as impossible and make decisions they are confident about. I guess if I had to put it in a nutshell to describe coaching and its power, I would say that coaching is a transformative partnership that allows individuals to discover their full potential, which will lead to both personal and professional growth, ultimately becoming the best version of themselves. It's truly amazing for both the coach and coachee.

Are there a few steps or tips you can give someone right now to start them on their transformation?

The most important thing is to be ready and willing for change. It is one thing to say you want to change, but that can be scary for some. The fear of the unknown and moving away from your comfort zone (i.e., the norm) is not always easy. However, if you consider everything that is possible and available to you when you step outside and grow, the opportunities are endless.

Find a coach that you are comfortable with, that you feel "gets" you, and that you can partner with on your remarkable journey and transformation. A great coaching collaboration can truly be life-changing, in the best of ways.

Do you have a gift/session that you can offer us?

Yes, access your free guide called, "Leading With Confidence; 5 Keys to Thriving in Your Leadership Role" on my website here: https://www.sidecarcoaching.com/freegift

About the Author
Joann Bellenkes

Joann Bellenkes is a Certified Executive and Leadership Coach, Organizational Development Coach, Trainer, and Speaker, known for her grounded approach and commitment to helping leaders excel. As the Founder of Sidecar Coaching, Joann focuses on fostering the confidence and authority of her clients, enabling them to inspire others and thrive in their leadership roles.

With over 25 years of corporate leadership experience, Joann's journey from seasoned executive to dedicated coach was driven by her passion for mentoring emerging leaders and guiding senior management. Her decision to pursue coaching full-time reflects her enduring dedication to personal and professional growth.

Joann holds a degree in Business and a Paralegal Certification from UCLA in Civil Litigation. She has earned three coaching certifications from the International Coach Federation (ICF) in Executive and Leadership Coaching, Organizational Development Coaching, and LIFE Coaching.

Elevate Your Life & Self Chapters

Turn Your Pain to Power

By Jewana White

"Pain is inevitable. Suffering is optional." ~Dalai Lama

Tell us about yourself, your expertise, and your coaching niche.

I'm Jewana White, the Midlife Resuscitator, reviving energetic wellness by raising your vibrational frequency and revolutionizing healthcare through self-care. My journey of transformation and resilience, shaped by personal traumas, has equipped me to guide women toward their internal power and true healing.

Through a unique system I've developed called CPR (Connecting, Processing, and Releasing), I address both physical and emotional imbalances, creating a harmonious balance of mind, body, and spirit. As a spiritual holistic intuitive teacher, I guide middle-aged women facing health crises or emotional overload to connect with themselves holistically and awaken to their true selves. By using energetic healing modalities such as Acupuncture, Reiki, Intuitive readings, and RTT Hypnotherapy, I help alleviate body aches, reduce stress, and restore the body's natural energy flow.

Tell us, what does coaching mean to you?

Coaching has been crucial in maintaining my mental health and life progression. As a young mother and wife, I felt overwhelmed and unhappy. Seeking help, I turned to the church, which led to significant trauma, or "church hurt." This combined with filing for bankruptcy and going through a divorce led me to therapy. While therapy helped me navigate the pain of my marriage breaking and subsequent divorce, it often focused on the problems rather than the solutions.

During this tumultuous period, it was the guidance from various teachers and coaches that allowed me to explore and understand myself on a deeper level, leading to true healing and growth. I've invested significantly in myself with multiple degrees, programs from coaches, and personal trainers for my goals. I recognized early on that without accountability and discipline, I struggle to show up for myself. Discipline is the consistency of actions. Setting goals is one thing; achieving them requires discipline, and coaching provides that discipline.

In your experience, what are some common misconceptions people have about coaching, and how do you address them to demonstrate its true value?

Many people underestimate the value of coaching, thinking they can navigate life's challenges alone. However, just as you would seek a doctor for physical ailments, a coach provides the expertise and support to help you overcome hurdles. There is someone in every area of life who has the experience and knowledge to help you grow.

One common misconception about coaching is that it costs too much. I always say, "You are your best investment. Tithe in yourself." Every dollar spent on your growth can multiply a hundredfold in value. Your health—whether mental, physical, or spiritual—is never too expensive to invest in.

Another misconception is that coaching is only for those who are struggling. It is for anyone looking to elevate their life, achieve their goals, and unlock their full potential.

The true value is, it is tailored to your unique needs, ensuring you achieve lasting success and fulfillment.

What kind of problems do you solve? Can you tell us a bit about the process that you walk people through?

Whether it's overcoming trauma, navigating life changes, or seeking personal growth, my process is centered around the CPR system: Connecting, Processing, and Releasing emotional and mental blocks, leading to true healing and empowerment.

Addressing pain and discomfort starts with recognizing that your feelings directly affect your body and overall well-being. Many people are unaware that their thoughts, words, and actions shape their reality. I help them connect with their true selves and understand this profound truth.

Next, we process these feelings, through various holistic and spiritual practices, we work on understanding and reframing these emotions and thoughts. Finally, we focus on releasing these blocks, allowing individuals to let go of what no longer serves them and embrace their innate power to create positive change. By recognizing and activating this power, they can transform their lives and achieve their desired outcomes.

Do you have a story about a client and how they achieved success with your coaching? Please give details.

Sarah was feeling completely overwhelmed and stuck in her life after a painful divorce and the relentless pressures of her job. Her health was deteriorating, and she felt emotionally exhausted. That's when she discovered my CPR system, and it changed everything for her. Today, she feels like a completely different person. She has a renewed sense of purpose, her health has improved, and she approaches life with a positive outlook. She's thriving both personally and professionally, and she owes it all to the powerful journey through my CPR system. It's truly a life-changing experience.

Did you go through the difficulties that you now help people with? Tell us about that and how it led you to become a coach.

I've faced my fair share of trauma. My journey began with my father's struggle with drug-induced schizophrenia. Imagine the confusion and fear of seeing your loving father transform from Mr. Rogers into Hulk Hogan without warning. Growing up in this chaotic environment was like walking on eggshells, never knowing what each day would bring.

Years later, I found myself in a marriage that added to my burdens. I was carrying the load, trying to keep our family afloat through bankruptcy and near foreclosure. The stress of our financial struggles was overwhelming, My health deteriorated as I juggled the roles of mother, wife, and breadwinner, all while feeling utterly alone. My husband of nearly 20 years watched my struggles without offering much support. The breaking point came when he said, "I know what it takes to make you happy; I just choose not to do it." Those words cut deep, leaving me feeling worthless and unloved. It was a soul-crushing moment that made me realize I had to choose myself if I wanted to survive.

From that moment on, I committed to "vibing up" from divorce, bankruptcy, foreclosure, and multiple surgeries. I embarked on a journey of intense healing, where I learned the profound truth that how I feel truly matters. I discovered that my thoughts, emotions, and physical sensations were all interconnected, and by addressing them, I could begin to heal.

This realization led to the creation of my business, U Factor Wellness. Every day, I had to remind myself, "You are a factor," to recognize my worth and value. It wasn't an easy path, but it was a necessary one. I had to learn to process and release the emotional and mental blocks that were holding me back.

These experiences have fueled my passion for helping others navigate similar challenges. I know firsthand the feelings of despair, isolation, and worthlessness. But I also know the incredible transformation that can occur when you choose yourself and commit to your well-being.

I hope to inspire others to recognize their worth and take the steps necessary to create a life filled with joy, health, and fulfillment. Together, we can transform your life and help you find the peace and happiness you deserve.

If someone were fearful of coaching, what would you tell them?

If you are not sure about coaching, I would tell you that having an external perspective is invaluable. Imagine being in a fog, unable to see clearly, and then someone with a lantern steps in, illuminating the path ahead. That's what a coach does, they bring light to the areas of your life that you can't see clearly.

A coach isn't just an outsider looking in; they provide a level of support that friends or spouses might not be able to offer, like challenging you or holding you accountable in the same way a coach can.

When your dreams and goals feel unsupported by those around you, it can be easy to lose focus and motivation. They help you maintain your momentum, especially when you start feeling overwhelmed or doubt creeps in. Your coach becomes your cheerleader, your strategist, and your accountability partner all rolled into one.

I know this firsthand. During my most challenging moments, it was my coaches who helped me stay on track. They were there when I felt like giving up, providing the support and guidance I needed to achieve my goals. Their presence made all the difference, helping me navigate through the fog and cross the finish line.

What would you tell someone who thinks they should be able to fix/solve this on their own?

I understand the belief that we should be able to handle everything on our own. I've been there, thinking I could shoulder all my burdens without assistance. However, I've learned that we activate a different type of power when we join forces with someone else. Coaching provides a unique blend of expertise, accountability, and encouragement that can transform your life.

Think of it like climbing a mountain. You might be able to make it to the top on your own, but having an experienced guide by your side helps you navigate the toughest paths, avoid pitfalls, and reach your destination more efficiently and safely. The guide's knowledge and support can make all the difference between a struggle and a successful ascent.

In my own life, I tried to manage everything alone until I realized the value of having a coach. Their guidance helped me see solutions I hadn't considered, offered new perspectives, and propelled me forward faster than I could have on my own. With a coach, I discovered strengths I didn't know I had and achieved goals that I once thought were out of reach.

Some believe having a coach is a sign of weakness; it's a power move toward personal empowerment and success. It's about recognizing that with the right support, you can unlock your full potential and create the life you truly desire.

How has being a coach and guiding others to empowerment influenced and changed your life?

Guiding others to realize their own power is profoundly soul-filling. There's nothing quite like witnessing someone's confidence blossom, seeing them embrace their true selves, and watching their body heal as their life choices begin to reflect their true value. I vividly remember one client who had constant pain and self-doubt. The journey was tough, but the moment she finally broke through was unforgettable. Her face lit up with a smile, her energy was renewed, and the positive changes in her life were undeniable. It was as if a heavy cloud had lifted, revealing the radiant person she always had the potential to be. Experiences like this continually inspire me and reinforce my commitment to helping others.

Each breakthrough, each smile, and each step forward in my clients' lives are testaments to the transformative power of coaching. These moments are the greatest rewards, filling my heart with immense joy and gratitude, and driving me to keep doing what I love.

What is the biggest takeaway about the power of coaching to remember?

One of my coaches always said, "People need people." I like to add, "People need positive people." Joining forces with a positive and empowering coach can create a ripple effect of positivity in your life. It's like having the cheat codes to the test of life, providing guidance and support, but it also accelerates your personal growth and helps you overcome obstacles more effectively.

Think of having a navigator on a long journey. You might reach your destination on your own, but with a navigator, you can take the best routes, avoid unnecessary detours, and arrive more efficiently and confidently. The positive influence of my coaches has been invaluable. Their insights and encouragement have propelled me to heights I never thought possible, and I will offer the same transformative experience to my clients.

Are there a few steps or tips you can give someone right now to start them on their transformation?

Here are a few steps to kickstart your transformation using my CPR system and the Vibe Up Checklist, which you can get from my website:

1. **C**hoose You and Your VIBE Every Day: Make a conscious decision every day to prioritize your well-being and maintain a positive vibrational frequency. Connecting with yourself.

2. **P**rocessing your self-belief. Have confidence in your abilities and your worth. Let go of past mistakes and recognize that everyone makes them. Use them as learning experiences. Trust that you have the strength and resilience to overcome challenges and achieve your goals.

3. **R**elease Positive Energy into Your Day: Start each day with "I am worthy of love and success," This sets a powerful intention for your day and helps align your actions with your desired outcomes.

Do you have a gift/session that you can offer us?

Download the Free Vibe Up Checklist at www.UFactorWellness.com to guide you on your journey. It's a valuable tool to stay connected, process your emotions, and release what no longer serves you. As an added gift, get a Free VIBE UP Call with me.

Remember, transformation starts with small, intentional steps. By choosing to prioritize your well-being and connecting with your true self, you can create a life filled with joy, health, and fulfillment. Download the Vibe Up Checklist today and start your journey with the support and guidance you deserve.

About the Author
Jewana White

Jewana White known as the "Midlife Resuscitator" is revolutionizing health care by bringing it back to self-care! Using her unique C.P.R system to revive energetic wellness, if you feel pain in the body, friction in relationships and in a hole financially, then there is STUCK ENERGY. Jewana uses a blend of Chinese medicine and spiritual practices in order to raise your natural healing energy to Avoiding Health Issues, Attracting more Love and creating more cash flow by aligning your VIBE

Her passion for living her best life is what began her spiritual journey. She attained a bachelor's degree in Biblical Studies and is an interfaith minister. She has an Associate degree in Massage Therapy, where she awoke to her power of energy healing, and is currently acquiring her Masters in Acupuncture, Chinese Medicine. She is a reiki master, a trained clairvoyant, and a Rapid Transformational Therapist.

It's Time For You

By Valerie J. Ritchie

"Embracing midlife is about reclaiming your power, finding your true self, and realising the journey of transformation is possible and profoundly empowering"

Tell us about yourself, your expertise, and your coaching niche.

Aloha, my name is Valerie Jacqueline Ritchie. I am an advocate and mentor for women in midlife, focusing on Self-Care, Self-Love, and Self-First. As a Midlife Empowerment Advocate, I am passionate about women's empowerment, personal growth, and embracing Divine Feminine energy. My niche centres on integrating the ancient yet timeless concepts of 'Crone Goddess' and 'Crone Wisdom' into modern discourse, presenting them as beacons of strength, grace, and empowerment.

My mission is to help women recognise themselves as embodiments of the Crone Goddess— figures of mature wisdom, power, and beauty. I encourage them to harness their Crone Wisdom, insights gained from a lifetime of rich experiences. My work aims to shift societal views, celebrate the richness of mature women's perspectives, and empower them to reclaim their roles in society. As the Voice of Joy, I exemplify the power of ageing gracefully and aim to demystify midlife.

Tell us, what does coaching mean to you?

Coaching to me is a sacred partnership. It's a deep connection between the coach and the client, a collaborative journey of self-discovery, empowerment, transition and transformation. Coaching provides the space to breathe and let go, making the biggest impact on one's life by feeling safe without judgement.

Coaching calls you to act, even when you don't know what or how. It's the first step where you can see potential and possibilities, and a time to unburden what was once held close.

Ultimately, coaching is about freedom. It guides you to be your true self, to explore, to travel, and to take on new adventures. It is flexible and fosters your sense of self-love and self-worth.

In your experience, what are some common misconceptions people have about coaching, and how do you address them to demonstrate its true value?

One common misconception is that coaching is only for those who are struggling, or failing, or for high performers, celebrities, and the wealthy. Many see it as a last resort rather than a proactive choice. Coaching is a resource for personal growth, regardless of one's journey.

Another misconception is that coaching is like therapy. While therapy delves into past traumas, coaching focuses on the present and the future, guiding clients to set and achieve their goals. A change in just a conversation can spark a lightbulb moment, demonstrating the true value of coaching. It's possible to have an amazing future, regardless of your past and present.

What kind of problems do you solve? Can you tell us a bit about the process that you walk people through?

As a coach specialising in transformative coaching for women in midlife, I address loss of identity, feeling unfulfilled, and navigating major life transitions, such as the physical impact of ageing, menopausal transition, career changes, shifts in family dynamics, or significant personal re-evaluations. My clients seek to rediscover joy and passion in their lives.

My process begins with a deep-dive session to understand the client's unique situation, dreams and goals. We then develop a personalised plan that includes goal setting, action steps, and regular check-ins to monitor progress. Throughout, I provide support, encouragement, and accountability.

I utilise a proprietary coaching model known as the Five R's: Reawaken, Reconnect, Realign, Rebalance, and Reclaim. This structured approach leads clients through a holistic journey of self-discovery, self-empowerment, and profound personal growth.

1. **Reawaken**: Focus on awakening dormant potentials and desires.
2. **Reconnect**: Rebuild bonds with their inner selves and loved ones.
3. **Realign**: Adjust life paths to harmonise with rediscovered values.
4. **Rebalance**: Establish equilibrium among all areas of life.
5. **Reclaim**: Take back control over their lives, assert their identity and step fully into their power.

Do you have a story about a client and how they achieved success with your coaching? Please give details.

At 58, Lisa, a former Director of Education, faced significant life challenges. Following a career setback due to restructuring, she struggled with her identity and purpose amid a menopausal transition. Lisa also dealt with a recent divorce and downsizing her home, leaving her feeling like a failure. We set goals for a healthier, more fulfilling path. She took up a remote job, alleviating stress.

With encouragement, Lisa embraced a growth mindset, recognising the importance of health and well-being. She re-educated herself about nutrition and began growing her own vegetables. Settling in an area surrounded by nature, she finds solace in daily walks with her dogs. This new lifestyle improved her physical, emotional, and mental well-being, showing that prioritising personal growth can lead to profound satisfaction and success.

Lisa's journey highlights how she transformed her approach to work and health, turning perceived failures into opportunities for development. Witnessing her growth was incredibly rewarding.

Did you go through the difficulties that you now help people with? Tell us about that and how it led you to become a coach.

I've faced my own midlife challenges, including a sense of loss and questioning my purpose. There was a time when I felt invisible and unsure of my next steps. Through my own journey of self-discovery and embracing Crone Wisdom, I found strength and clarity. This ignited my passion to help other women navigate similar transitions. Over a decade marked by a series of major traumatic losses, I experienced heartbreak and devastation. It began with the news that I was 'postmenopausal' at 42, shattering my dreams of motherhood. This was followed by a hysterectomy, the loss of five loved ones, redundancy, and the end of my marriage.

These experiences not only led me to pursue a career in coaching but also deeply informed my approach to helping others navigate similar paths. I realised that society often overlooks the wisdom and value of women in midlife. This realisation spurred me to challenge these narratives and embrace my own worth. Overcoming the fear of being unheard taught me the importance of self-love and advocacy. I help my clients see their worth and potential, no matter their age.

A pivotal moment came during a midlife re-evaluation. Like many women I support, I questioned my career and the authenticity of my life. This period of introspection was challenging but necessary for genuine happiness.

For instance, frustrations with a younger manager and a lack of stimulation led me to reconsider my career. Simultaneously, the deaths of close family members heightened my awareness of mortality, urging me to live more fully. This emphasised the importance of health— physical, emotional, mental and spiritual— and reshaped my priorities.

My midlife re-evaluation taught me the value of living a life aligned with one's values. I encourage my clients to explore and define authenticity and help them to align their lives accordingly. Having experienced the empowerment that comes from taking control of one's life, I emphasise actionable strategies in my coaching.

If someone were fearful of coaching, what would you tell them?

It is natural to feel apprehensive about starting something as personal as coaching. Coaching is about support and growth, not judgment. It's an opportunity to invest in oneself and gain clarity. I would encourage you to take that first step with an open mind. Every great journey begins with a single step. It is just a conversation.

If you're feeling fearful or uncertain, know that these feelings are valid and common. Change can be daunting, but as a coach, my role is to support, not judge. We work together at a comfortable pace, and every step is designed with your needs in mind.

The coaching environment is a safe space everything shared is confidential, allowing you to explore your thoughts and feelings without fear.

I would share how coaching has helped others who might have been skeptical or fearful but found profound value in the process. Whether it's gaining clearer insight making meaningful life changes, or feeling more empowered, the benefits can be significant.

For those particularly nervous, I suggest starting with a short initial consultation. This low-pressure introduction allows you to ask questions and get a feel for how coaching can help, without a full commitment. Often, the greatest growth comes from stepping beyond your comfort zone.

What would you tell someone who thinks they should be able to fix/solve this on their own?

Many of us pride ourselves on our independence, often imposed by societal expectations. It's understandable to feel you should handle challenges on your own. While self-reliance is admirable, we all need guidance and perspective at times. This isn't a sign of weakness; it's a sign of strength and wisdom. Coaching provides an objective viewpoint and tailored strategies that can accelerate your progress. Even the most successful people rely on the expertise of others. Just as athletes work with coaches to enhance their performance, a life coach can optimise your personal growth and help you navigate challenges more effectively. It's natural to have blind spots—areas we cannot see clearly. As a coach, I offer a fresh, unbiased perspective that can reveal new possibilities.

While it's possible to resolve challenges independently, coaching can significantly speed up the process. It provides focused strategies and tools tailored to your specific needs, helping you achieve your goals more quickly and effectively than through trial and error alone. One of the key benefits of coaching is the accountability it provides. Having a coach to hold you accountable and cheer you on makes a substantial difference.

Sometimes, the hardest thing is to allow ourselves to receive help. Encouraging self-compassion means recognising that you deserve support, and seeking help is a proactive step towards self-care. Finally, I invite you to explore what's possible with coaching. It's a strategic choice for anyone serious about making meaningful changes.

How has being a coach and guiding others to empowerment influenced and changed your life?

Being a coach makes me smile; it's not just a profession—it's a journey of continual learning and personal growth. It has deepened my understanding of human resilience and the power of empathy. This role intertwines with the skills I obtained from over 30 years in education. Witnessing the positive changes in my clients' lives is incredibly fulfilling and motivates me to continue this work. Coaching has enriched my life with purpose and a sense of contribution to the well-being of others.

It has compelled me to continuously evaluate my perspectives and assumptions. This ongoing self-reflection has made me more effective in helping others and led to greater self-awareness and clarity in my own life. Through my clients' stories, my capacity for empathy has expanded, enriching my personal relationships. Appreciating my own resilience mirrors the human capacity for change and growth I see in my clients. This strengthens my resolve and reminds me that it's never too late to embrace new beginnings.

It's a privilege to play a role in someone else's journey of empowerment, and each success story adds to a sense of accomplishment that is deeply gratifying. As a lifelong learner, I practice what I preach. Guiding others towards living their best lives constantly reminds me to live mine to the fullest, embrace challenges, and continually seek growth and fulfilment.

What is the biggest takeaway about the power of coaching to remember?

Coaching is a catalyst for transformation. It empowers individuals to see beyond their limitations and tap into their true potential. Coaching cultivates self-awareness, accountability, ownership and resilience, enabling my clients to navigate challenges with confidence and clarity. It's a powerful tool for creating lasting, positive change.

Are there a few steps or tips you can give someone right now to start them on their transformation?

Here are three practical steps you can take right now to set the foundation for meaningful change:

1. **Cultivate Self-Awareness**: Understand your current state, including your strengths, weaknesses, desires, and fears. Spend time reflecting on your life and feelings. Journaling can help increase self-awareness and clarify your thoughts and emotions.

2. **Create a Vision Board**: Collect images, quotes, and symbols that represent your goals and aspirations. Place your vision board somewhere you can see it every day to keep your objectives top of mind and stir positive emotions.

3. **Prioritise Self-Care**: Ensure you are taking care of your physical, emotional and mental health by getting enough sleep, eating well, exercising, and engaging in relaxation practices like meditation or yoga. Self-care is essential for sustaining your journey toward change.

By following these steps, you can begin to make meaningful changes that will propel you towards your personal and professional goals. Remember, transformation is a journey, not a race. Take it one step at a time and celebrate your progress along the way.

Do you have a gift/session that you can offer us?

As a token of appreciation and to support you on your journey, I am offering a complimentary 30-minute **Discover Your Crone Goddess** conversation. During this session, we will explore your current challenges, identify your goals, and create a personalised action plan to kickstart your transformation.

www.TransformationInAction.CoachesConsole.com/Calendar

Also, grab my free guide **Gratitude Journaling Sprint Challenge** so you can embark on a transformative seven-day journey to cultivate joy and appreciation in your daily life.

www.TransformationInAction.CoachesConsole.com/Gratitude

About the Author
Valerie J. Ritchie

Valerie Jacqueline Ritchie stands at the forefront of a movement redefining the essence of midlife for women. With an unwavering belief in the principles of Self-Care, Self-Love, and placing Self-First, she champions the journey of self-discovery and empowerment that women embark upon in their midlife years. Valerie introduces the ancient yet timeless concepts of 'Crone Goddess' and 'Crone Wisdom' into modern discourse, presenting them as beacons of strength, grace, and empowerment for the contemporary woman.

With a Master of Science in Health Sciences, Valerie's mission is to illuminate the path for women to embrace these powerful identities within themselves, helping them recognise that they are the embodiments of the Crone Goddess—a revered and majestic figure of mature wisdom, power, and beauty, deserving of deep admiration and respect. This identity encourages them to harness their Crone Wisdom, the invaluable insights gained from a lifetime of rich experiences. Her voice is a testament to the power of ageing gracefully, crafting a new lexicon for redefining midlife.

Finding Your Authentic Self

By Susie Procini

"Only when we are brave enough to explore the darkness will we discover the infinite power of our light." ~Brene Brown

Tell us about yourself, your expertise, and your coaching niche.

Over the past 25 years, I began a journey to discover who I was and what I was meant to do. I am a Women's Empowerment Coach. I teach and guide women of all ages to find who they are from the inside out and to discover the purpose and passion they are being called to step into. The importance of this for me was to be able to discover who I was without the conditioning; the learning I received as a young child. It allowed me to think on my own without anyone defining who I was.

Tell us, what does coaching mean to you?

Coaching is a means of learning how to do things differently. When we are growing up in our families, we are learning what is important in our family unit. We do it "this way" because our families have always done it "this way". However, as we grow and go out into the world, we see there are many ways of doing things, not just one way.

Working with a coach gives you the privilege of agency to do things differently. Just because you have always done it that way does not mean it serves you as you mature. Coaching allows us to see ourselves in ways we might not have seen ourselves in our families. For example, I was very shy as a child. Now I see that I can have a conversation with anyone at any time. I learned a sense of confidence and assuredness I didn't have growing up. Coaching has taught me how to see all of the possibilities I have to choose from in how I want to live my life.

In your experience, what are some common misconceptions people have about coaching, and how do you address them to demonstrate its true value?

People have a misconception that coaching is like therapy. They also think the coaches are going to tell them what they need to do. Coaching is a collaboration and a partnership between the coach and the client. A coach helps the client understand the conditioning that they have learned growing up. The coach then guides the client to different ways of seeing or behaving in order to receive a different and better outcome. You can call it unlearning behaviors.

When I am coaching a client, I ask them how she would like to do things differently. I also often share what I am doing differently because of the coaching I received. I did not know how to have an argument with my husband. When we would argue, I would continue battling until my husband would see it my way. This could take hours and hours and it would become very heated. There was a lot of yelling and screaming. It was exhausting and it did not bring us any closer in our relationship. How am I now doing this differently? I learned that we could have a conversation about what we were experiencing without yelling and screaming, and he didn't have to see it my way. We could agree to disagree and come to an amicable resolution. We could share how we were feeling AND I didn't have to take things personally.

What kind of problems do you solve? Can you tell us a bit about the process that you walk people through?

One of the biggest problems I help women work on is their increased belief and confidence in who they are. This allows them to enjoy knowing and loving themselves at a very deep level. Women are natural-born nurturers. They help others instinctively. In that process, it's easy for them to forget about who they are. My process of guiding clients to the greatest self-discovery of who they are, allows them to take the time to be with themselves. Setting aside time to be with themselves alone and to care for themselves is a practice I help women begin to cultivate in their lives. It is important to go within and quiet the external world in order to find and discover their true authentic selves.

Do you have a story about a client and how they achieved success with your coaching? Please give details.

I have a client who is a high-achieving professional who has her own architectural firm. She is a wife and a mother of three children. When she was growing up in Italy, she was always taught to work hard, grind it out, achieve as much as possible and do, do and do. She came to a point where it was all too much. She needed to find a work-life balance. When I asked her what she loved, she had a very hard time finding the answer. There had been no focus on who she was, the focus was more on what she could achieve.

We began a practice of meditation and journaling to get her more in touch with her inner self. She started taking baby steps towards her goals. Taking baby steps consistently over time will always reap huge gains. Now, the awareness and the confidence she has developed in herself, with her work, and with her family life provides the balance and fulfillment she had been searching for. She made changes within her family and work structure to support everything she was doing, and now being it and doing it with ease.

Did you go through the difficulties that you now help people with? Tell us about that and how it led you to become a coach.

I teach women from my own personal experience, the lessons I have learned, and the way to create a life of happiness, contentment, and ease. I realize that the difficulties I went through in my life are the lessons I needed to learn in order to create the life I love. One of the biggest lessons I have learned is not to take things personally. I used to always make what someone said about me to be true and took it very personally. It was through taking things personally that I realized I did this because I did not believe in myself enough and did not know who I was to be able to say, "That is not true."

When you know yourself so deeply, you can stand up to another and declare, "I do not believe that is true." Then, there is no need to defend yourself or make another person see your point of view. When you know yourself so deeply, you can respond in your power and truth and be okay.

This profound realization led me first to become a health and wellness coach. I had a coach myself, and it allowed me to see there were so many things I didn't even know I could do differently. I could see with the eyes of my coach that there were so many ways to deal with situations in life that would make it easier. I could respond instead of reacting.

It was through health coaching and working with women that I saw the women I was coaching had so many other issues that needed healing before they could get to know how they were fueling their bodies. My life coach asked me, "What do you love most about health coaching?" I responded, "I love seeing women unfold like a rose bud that is blooming, opening up petal by petal, and finding who they really are." My coach suggested I look to pivoting into empowerment coaching for women and I am so very happy I did!

I am a woman who grew up in a family that was in survival mode. For me, the oldest of three children, I took to a people-pleasing role. I wanted to make everyone happy, and I made it my job to take care of everyone. In doing that job, I never really thought much about myself and my own happiness. It was a job that a 12-year-old had no business taking on. If I didn't know who I was, how could I care for others?

I got married when I was 28 years old and kept the job of taking care of others in place. Everyone benefited from my role, except myself. When I had two children, my job expanded to taking care of them and all of their needs. This isn't a bad job unless you lose yourself in the doing.

When my youngest child went off to college, I realized my job of doing for everyone else was coming to an end. What the heck was I going to do with myself? When I spoke that question out loud, my husband said I could come back and work for him. And it was in that moment it felt like a lightning bolt struck me and I could hear "There is something out there for you to do for YOU!!!

Wow!!! I knew in that moment I was now on a journey to do something that would fulfill me. But who was I? What did I want to do? Thus began the journey to discover who I was and what I was being called to do.

The pivotal moment in my life that had me pursue coaching was the thought of how I had helped everyone else in my life achieve their dreams, and I was happy to do so, but when I was looking at an empty nest in my own life, I felt that sense of emptiness in myself and in my life ahead. I realized that if I was not on a continuous discovery as to who I was and what I desired to create for myself, I was just an empty vessel. At 72 years-old now, I am living my best life. It is never too late to go after a dream, goal, or vision, and we never have to listen to anyone tell us we can't.

If someone were fearful of coaching, what would you tell them?

If someone was fearful about coaching and making the necessary changes in their lives, I would say, listen and trust your heart, your intuition, and your higher guidance. No matter what that looks like for you, that guidance would never give you anything that would be of harm to you. Take the changes in the smallest steps. That will have you keeping your brain calm and prevent it from going into fight or flight mode. When you have a coach walking right beside you on the journey, there is nothing to fear.

What would you tell someone who thinks they should be able to fix/solve this on their own?

Wouldn't that be great if we could do it that way? However, we can't because the only thing we have to draw from in our brain is our own past experiences. Since our own past experiences have gotten us to a place of frustration and unhappiness, we truly need someone else, a coach, who has gone through the transformation process in order to learn there is a different way to deal with life's situations. You may think it is hard to change, but it can't be any harder than what you are experiencing now.

How has being a coach and guiding others to empowerment influenced and changed your life?

As much as I have gone through the transformation process, I am only a few steps ahead of my clients. I can now fast-track them to the life they desire more quickly. This is what I teach to my clients and receive so much more from them. The women I work with are amazing human beings and they give back to me so much more. I also know that I can only teach them what I am learning. That keeps me on a constant path of evolution for myself and ultimately my clients. It is a journey I will be on for the rest of my life. It is so fulfilling, and I know every day, I am living and serving in my purpose and passion.

What is the biggest takeaway about the power of coaching to remember?

The biggest takeaway about the power of coaching is that if you are unhappy with whom you are or with your life, then you can do something about it. You don't have to sit with your feeling of being alone or not feeling good enough. There are coaches out there who will support you in getting back on your feet. And, if you are dedicated to doing the real work, you will be a whole new you.

Are there a few steps or tips you can give someone right now to start them on their transformation?

Yes. You don't have to stay stuck. It is all in your control. Talk to someone who has a coach and receive some feedback from them. Begin to search on the internet for someone you feel aligned with and have a call with them to see if you are a good fit for each other.

Here are some tips to start your transformation right now:

- Be aware that this is going to be an inside job. That means going
- within yourself.
- Begin by journaling how you are feeling or what you want to do differently.
- Inquire to your Higher Power asking "What is my best next step?
- Start a meditation practice. There are many free meditation apps to choose from. Having a place of stillness and silence allows you to access your intuition.

Do you have a gift/session that you can offer us?

I have a complimentary clarity call to uncover your personalized strategies for growth and empowerment. Schedule here: www.EmpoweredFromTheHeart.com.

About the Author
Susie Procini

Susie Procini began her life coach for women practice 15 years ago when she became certified as a health and wellness coach. She attended the Institute for Integrative Nutrition. It was during her time as a health and wellness coach that she continually saw a pattern that kept repeating when she was working with her women clients.

Most of her women clients were so burdened with limiting beliefs and patterns they had carried for so many years. It was then that Susie saw a great need, a need that was not being met, that she pivoted her focus and began her work as a life coach for women.

Why life coach for women? Susie has been on her own personal transformational journey for over 20 years. She has consistently done the work to change the way she had been living, releasing limiting beliefs and old patterns and growing into the woman she desired. She is still on the personal growth journey and she is committed to doing the real work so she can help her clients to grow and transform, fostering a sense of women empowerment.

A Paradigm Shift

By India Willis

"You can focus on things that are barriers or you can focus on scaling the wall or redefining the problem." ~Tim Cook

Tell us about yourself, your expertise, and your coaching niche.

As the CEO and founder of Life Activated Consulting Services, I'm making a difference by empowering women to achieve their fullest potential through personalized coaching. I serve as a Life Resource Strategist, with expertise as a Certified Life Harmony Coach, Emotional Intelligence Expert, and Keynote Speaker. Through my coaching practice, I offer a blend of biblical wisdom and practical principles to support women in their journey towards self-improvement.

Tell us, what does coaching mean to you?

Coaching and mentoring; it is a part of who I am as a person. Women want to unburden themselves, to unlock mysteries hidden deep in their heart. They're searching for something or someone who can help shine the light in the right direction. Coaching provides the hand-holding, while the individual embraces a new journey of self-discovery.

I believe the key to achieving success for women, is through a holistic approach: identifying emotional barriers and unhealthy trends that lead to paralysis and stagnation. Stagnation, as a silent barrier, can be a mental and physical death agent. I recognized stagnation in my own life, which led me to hire the services of a business coach.

What I didn't know about coaching is this: coaches don't tell you what you should be doing, but instead, they lead you out of an emotional fog so that you can discover what is already in front and inside of you. Through my own self-discovery journey, my eyes were opened to fulfilling a niche for women wanting to transition into their lives.

In your experience, what are some common misconceptions people have about coaching, and how do you address them to demonstrate its true value?

One common misconception is the belief that coaching is another form of mentoring. There's a difference to each approach. While mentoring provides advice and answers, coaching doesn't give you solutions. Instead, you are guided to discover answers for yourself. Coaching has clear goals, time limits, and mutual accountabilities, whereas mentoring tends to be more informal, and open-ended and may be contracted for longer periods of time.

Women may shy away from coaching as there may be the assumption that coaching is only for individuals who are struggling or facing challenges. This is far from the truth! Coaching benefits high-performing individuals, those seeking self-improvement, the homemaker seeking organization skills, those transitioning through a life event such as a divorce, and so on.

A third misconception people believe is that coaching requires a considerable time commitment. On the contrary, effective coaching doesn't necessarily mean lengthy sessions. Coaching is an investment in your professional or personal development and life transitions. The time spent with a coach is valuable time worth spending, especially if you are seeking to achieve more peace and clarity in your life.

What kind of problems do you solve? Can you tell us a bit about the process that you walk people through?

As a Life Resource Strategist, I navigate individuals through the most uncomfortable stages in their lives.

- The single mom who's struggling to balance her life, work and children while holding onto her sanity.
- The professional woman frustrated with the lack of professional growth and promotional opportunities with her current employer.
- The wife who is struggling with communication issues within her marriage.
- The entrepreneur who requires accountability for a business venture.
- The caregiver who needs support and guidance while caring for a loved one.

No matter the stage of life or struggles women are facing, the coaching process begins with the end in mind. An individual must be willing to release negative emotions, embrace the truth of the situation and give themselves permission to grieve in a healthy way.

The walls we build around ourselves often have story labels attached such as family trauma, relationship trauma, job/career dissatisfaction and so forth. We try to guard ourselves and our hearts from the very thing, entity or people that may cause us discomfort to the point of pain. We often fail, masking the hurt or pain until it becomes all-consuming. How do you begin to move past the pain that somehow penetrated through to the soul?

I personally know that the walls built up in our lives are scalable. Walls can be removed brick by brick, scaled over entirely or can be broken down with a sledgehammer. The technique utilized to scale a wall in life depends on the depth of the issue being explored and how rapidly you want to move forward, beyond the stigma of paralysis.

My coaching practice is based on the Scaling W.A.L.L.S method with this simple principle: If you are provided tangible and achievable steps to reduce overwhelm, you will scale those walls holding you back from experiencing more clarity and ease in life. Each phase within the Scaling W.A.L.L.S method is necessary to progress through because the focus is a holistic approach.

In the physical sense, no one can scale a natural wall by just thinking about it! Actionable and functional steps are uniquely formulated so that what seems impossible to the individual is now more simplified and achievable. My clients overcome emotional barriers and stagnation as they progress through the five phases of Scaling W.A.L.L.S:

- **W**ake-up the current mindset, scale stagnation:
- **A**chieve clarity, what is holding you back from moving forward
- **L**et go, embrace tranquility, scale all emotions
- **L**earn to leverage time wisely - scale your time
- **S**eek to sustain success – scale new possibilities

Do you have a story about a client and how they achieved success with your coaching? Please give details.

The following story I am about to share debunks the misconception that coaching takes a lot of time and commitment. My client is a divorced woman caring for her only child, who is now in her early twenties. In our first session, she talked quite a bit about her daughter's anxiety with school, health issues and overwhelm, even while being in their home that once was shared with both parents. Her daughter experienced much depression. As a coach, you don't bring judgment into the session, rather use the discovery time to assess what questions need to be asked to steer the conversation. The single question I asked the client during phase I was: "What does your daughter see when she spends time with you?"

After a brief pause, my client realized that her daughter perceived anxiety, worry, and overwhelm—emotions she herself was experiencing. Unbeknownst to her, her emotional state functioned as a conduit, linking her daughter's behavior by association. This dynamic exemplifies codependency in their relationship. Further exploration revealed that my client's own emotional well-being directly impacted her daughter's state of mind. This revelation proved paralyzing for both. However, as my client awakened to her current mindset and released negative emotions, she embarked on a new journey of forward movement, determined to approach things differently.

Weeks later, my client let me know she took a trip by herself while her daughter stayed with friends for a few days. She had returned refreshed and energized. Taking the trip by herself was daunting, but she found enjoyment in the solo trip. My client experienced a paradigm shift in her thinking, opening the pathway for transformation to occur.

Did you go through the difficulties that you now help people with? Tell us about that and how it led you to become a coach.

My experiences may not look like someone else's experience, but ultimately, we are all challenged with how we overcome obstacles put in our path. I draw my experiences from relationships: Spouse, children, siblings, parents, co-workers, friends, acquaintances, business partners, and even church members (church hurt). There is nothing new under the sun, only different people.

They say your gifting makes room for you. No matter where I lived or worked (I moved several times), my office or cubicle became a revolving place for people to come and sit, seek advice, and/or unburden themselves. I became a safe place for people and was given the beautiful gift of insight and wisdom for those individuals. I had already operated in the role of a coach and mentor before I ever officially identified myself as one.

In October of 2017, I experienced a career-changing event that paralyzed me, not physically, but emotionally. I was uncertain as to which direction I should take. The overwhelm, fear, and anxiety (sound familiar?) almost took me down.

My department was downsized in the blink of an eye. Certifications, promotions, and positions no longer mattered. I went from an analyst one day, to a call center customer service representative in the same week. That life-changing event was the best and the worst thing that could happen to me all at once. The change may have been completely unexpected, however, it catapulted me into a new world called freedom. I fired my boss (literally) and became a full-fledged entrepreneur for the first time. I had a lot to learn, yet I was determined.

I serve a mighty God who knows all about me and my struggles. I refused to allow a corporation to dictate my life so much that I was about to lose hope and settle into a mindset of fear. All I can say is, but God! My faith was tested in those days, and I have never looked back with regret or remorse. It was the end of one chapter and the beginning of something new.

I have coached and mentored hundreds of women throughout my corporate career. Now I continue my coaching as an entrepreneur with the amazing opportunity to impact thousands of women every day. I love living a fully activated life!

If someone were fearful of coaching, what would you tell them?

Coaching is simply allowing someone else to provide support and guidance in their current journey or situation. We all can relate to being a first-time driver behind the wheel of a car, so I use this analogy: You are the driver, and the coach is the passenger. As a driver, you sit in your seat with real anxieties, real-life issues or problems, and you desire to move out of those emotions into a safety zone. The biggest leap of faith you could take is to trust the knowledge and experience of a coach, your passenger. As the driver, you cannot get to where you want to go until you move the car from park to drive. In other words, let the stirring inside you lead you to act over any fears that may keep you stuck. Once faith is exercised, relief and hope take over. Clients often express to me that they wish they had taken the leap so much sooner.

What would you tell someone who thinks they should be able to fix/solve this on their own?

We all think we are more than capable of solving our own problems until the situation becomes unbearable or appears unsolvable. To the individual who feels confident they can manage their own problems, kudos! I wish them the absolute best and truly hope forward movement is on the horizon. However, coaching could provide the assistance of moving away the fog, opening the door to self-discovery and establishing of a clear path of direction sooner rather than later. I may ask a couple of thought-provoking questions, "How long have you dealt with this situation?" and/or "How long do you think it will take you to solve it for yourself?" The answers may vary, and, in the end, they recognize it's not a bad idea to seek out assistance because they are so tired of spinning on the hamster wheel.

How has being a coach and guiding others to empowerment influenced and changed your life?

I was in a place and time in my life where I didn't know what I was missing until I had a paradigm shift in my own thinking. I worked hard for over 25 years for a corporation, coaching others personally and professionally without even a thought of working for myself. Now I am where I am supposed to be, doing what I love to do.

When I see light bulb moments, actionable steps embarked upon and lives changed for the better, it brings me so much joy! I experience a purpose being fulfilled in my life every time I meet with a client or facilitate a group coaching session. Coaching changes lives, therefore, I am a conduit for changing lives. When one woman is positively impacted, everyone in her sphere of influence is impacted for the better. I call that impact, the power of duplication.

What is the biggest takeaway about the power of coaching to remember?

Coaching can be the stimulus for launching a life-changing transformation. I would not be in the business of coaching if I had not hired a personal coach myself. The journey was insightful, evoking emotions to rise to the surface I had buried for years. The guidance I received illuminated my own self-discovery path towards becoming a life coach.

Are there a few steps or tips you can give someone right now to start them on their transformation?

A personal transformation can be a profound shift in one's mindset, behavior, or life goals leading to growth and self-improvement. Transformation can represent a powerful force for reshaping your life, relationships, and surroundings and even opening your eyes to a deeper understanding of the world.

Here are three steps that anyone can implement today:

- Assess, self-evaluate your current situation and any associated emotions:
    - Are your emotions negative, positive, or indifferent?
    - Do your emotions have you paralyzed or are you freely moving forward?
- Think about what you are thinking about. Thoughts can be all-consuming.
    - Capture your thoughts and examine if they are self-serving or destructive.
    - If it fits into the latter, immediately cast it out.
    - Your thoughts feed into your emotions and emotions

can feed into your thoughts.

- Lastly, make the ultimate decision to change your life. It's not a "how" decision but a "when" decision. When you decide to transform your life:
    - Start journaling, keep a record of what led you to take this powerful step.
    - Tell someone you trust to hold you accountable so that you can keep moving forward.
    - Allow yourself to grieve the past and then embrace the future you.

Do you have a gift/session that you can offer us?

I have created an Empowerment Blueprint that is easily adaptable for anyone to use to start a transformation journey. A blueprint is a roadmap that leads you to your ultimate destination. You can download a copy from my website at

www.lifeactivatedconsultingservices.org/blueprint

About the Author
India Willis

India Willis became the CEO of Life Activated Consulting Services in October of 2018, after spending 25 years in Corporate America. As a Life Resource Strategist, she is in pursuit of helping women worldwide to create mission-driven paths for purposeful living. By utilizing her years of accumulated experience in mentoring, coaching, and community service, India sought to serve women by inspiring them to live an activated life on their own terms. India is a certified Emotional Intelligence expert and Life Harmony Coach.

India is highly sought after as a facilitator, speaker and trainer for various events, virtually and in-person presented by the organization and within her community. India also fuels her passion as a leader in Women's Ministry within her local church. She volunteers her time and talents as a coach and mentor, providing foundational and spiritual principles to women seeking to increase their faith through everyday circumstances that may arise. It is India's heart to inspire women globally to reset their thinking, restore peace and tranquility, then rise into their greatness!

Shining Your Light

By Alyssa Utecht

"The day she let go of the things that were weighing her down was the day she began to shine the brightest."
~Katrina Mayer

Tell us about yourself, your expertise, and your coaching niche.

I am a transformational coach and intuitive guide. I am here to uplift and empower women. I assist people who feel a sense of discontent with their lives, even when they "should" be happy. I help those who feel pulled in a hundred directions at once, with too much on their plates, who can't figure out how to lighten their load. I support women who KNOW there is more available: more joy, more wealth, more vibrant health, more ease, more love.

We look at what is keeping you stuck—in your health, wealth, and/or your relationships. We clear out everything that is no longer serving you and heal what is holding you back so that you can love yourself and your life more.

This leads to more confidence in yourself and your choices. You'll find more fulfillment in your current job…or be inspired to follow your passion. Taking care of yourself will be more enjoyable. Your relationships will feel more fluid and more loving. You'll find you have unwavering boundaries in challenging situations. Money will begin to flow in. And many areas of your life will just seem easier.

Tell us, what does coaching mean to you?

The word coach will mean different things to different people. Coaches are available for sports performance, business, finances, health, acting, voice, parenting, and even shopping (think stylist.) A coach is someone who guides, supports, pushes, encourages, and makes sure you don't feel alone in your desire and effort to reach a goal and change your life. The greatest asset a good coach has, in any field, is the ability to shine a light on a situation. As an objective observer, a coach can see things the client cannot-limiting beliefs, patterns of sabotage, hidden agendas, and much more.

In your experience, what are some common misconceptions people have about coaching, and how do you address them to demonstrate its true value?

I know there are many coaches working in the world today. It feels like the field has grown very quickly. This is amazing! So many of us have struggled alone for so long, and I believe we are getting more comfortable asking for help. (Well, some of us.) That said, there is a part of the general population that might scoff at having a life coach or a health coach. That's okay, too. Not everyone needs or wants support. However, hiring a coach, someone who is an expert in their field, will absolutely support you reaching your goals more quickly and more easily....and hopefully with a lot more joy. That gives you more time and energy for the people you want to spend time with, doing the things you love to do. I encourage people to invest in themselves. The cost of not taking action is more of the same.

What kind of problems do you solve? Can you tell us a bit about the process that you walk people through?

I can assist clients with financial struggles, inability to reach goals, overwhelm and stress, troublesome relationships, binge eating, feeling unclear about their purpose, or simply a lack of joy, and more. When meeting someone who's interested in working with me, the first thing we do is sit down for a heart-to-heart. We take an hour to get really clear about what isn't working in their life and how long it's been an issue. I ask direct, insightful questions to help unpack what's going on underneath. Maybe there is a lot of tension in your household. Maybe you wake up in the night with racing thoughts and can't get back to sleep. Or no matter how hard you work, you just can't seem to make enough money to get out of debt. Perhaps, you sit down in front of the TV in the evening and before you realize it, you've eaten an entire bag of chips. It could be any combination of challenges. You may know that you don't want more of the same, but you have no idea how to access something different.

We use the conversation to get to know one another. If both parties feel like it's a good fit, I'll make a recommendation for how we might begin the healing process. Then, we jump in right away. Having a coach is great because if you put in the effort, you can build momentum quickly and the shifts will soon follow. Typically, after working with me, my clients say they feel calmer and steadier. They notice they are no longer triggered by the things that used to irritate them. They can suddenly interact with a difficult co-worker or demanding family member without getting angry or feeling powerless. They make healthy choices, and it has suddenly become easy! Others note that their household has become more harmonious, and they report feeling more joyful as they go about their day.

Do you have a story about a client and how they achieved success with your coaching? Please give details.

I have a client who struggled with money for most of her life. She knew she was meant for financial abundance and worked very hard without sustained success. She owned rental properties for one source of income, which kept her afloat until her new business took off. She had quit her "day job" but owed a year's worth of unpaid bills to the utility company. She had tried to pay it several times, but they just kept putting her off. They were restructuring and told her to wait. She felt very stressed because she didn't have the money to pay it all at once.

Finally, she called one last time, and an employee from the utility company said her entire bill was forgiven. A government assistance program had covered the entire thing! The total was more than $13,000 and she didn't have to pay anything! She was stunned and delighted. This happened within a month of us doing deep work on her money story and clearing out limiting beliefs. (She also met the "Love of Her Life" about 6 months later. Just a side effect of our consistent work together.)

Another client had a fixation with white chocolate. It reminded her of her mother, and she realized she would turn to it when she felt lonely, sad, or stressed. She always had some with her and reached for it frequently. We dove deep and uncovered what was really going on under the craving. We cleared out the old memories and stuck energies, and she has not craved white chocolate for 6 months and counting.

Did you go through the difficulties that you now help people with? Tell us about that and how it led you to become a coach.

I've been extremely sensitive all my life. I can feel other people's anger and stress. I can sense their grief and desperation. Unconsciously, I took many of these emotions on as my own. My mood would quickly shift as my personal balance was thrown off. This led to me feeling anxious and hyper-vigilant for much of my life—even as a young child. Over the years, that developed into mental, emotional, and physical health challenges. After years of searching and trying everything, cutting myself off from the world more and more, I learned about the mind/body connection.

Once I realized my thoughts and emotions were directly tied to my physical well-being, I found myself on my own healing journey. As I filled up my giant toolbox full of invaluable tools, I slowly became aware that I was meant to help other women through their pain and suffering and to the other side. I've been on both sides of that river. It takes some effort to swim across, and on the other side lies more ease, joy, and freedom every single day. Now, I see my sensitivity as my greatest gift, and I am honored to use it to help others.

If someone were fearful of coaching, what would you tell them?

I have total compassion for someone who feels fearful of coaching. It can feel very vulnerable to go to a stranger, tell them your deepest desires, dreams, and fears, and then have a discussion with them about why you don't have what you want yet. Maybe they have had a coach and it did not really work out—they didn't reach their goal or couldn't connect with that person. As humans, it doesn't always feel safe to really go for it, especially if we've tried and tried before.

I would encourage that person/you to find a quiet place, take some deep breaths, close your eyes, and simply sit for a few minutes. Think about what it is they/you truly want. Then, as they/you go through their/your days, be curious and open to what pops up on their/your radar. Do they/you see an ad for a YouTube video on the subject they're/you're interested in? Maybe a friend mentions a coach who has started a practice in their/your area. It's possible they'll/you'll receive an email talking about the exact thing they/you long for. If we give ourselves the time to tune in, our intuition will lead us to the right first step. A coach/client relationship needs to be a good fit. Don't feel bad about taking the time to search for a great coach for YOU.

What would you tell someone who thinks they should be able to fix/solve this on their own?

If I were having a conversation with someone who was really struggling, I'd ask a lot of questions (because that's what I do!) How long have you struggled? Who else in your life has been affected? What has been the cost? If it's been a challenge in your life for a few weeks or months, I'd say, "Go for it!" However, if it has been something you have spent years trying to "fix", I would encourage you to consider reaching out for support. With a coach, you will reach your goals more quickly, more easily, and will have the continual support of someone who cares.

How has being a coach and guiding others to empowerment influenced and changed your life?

Being a coach completely fills my soul with love and gratitude. I have spent my life lifting others up--that will always be a part of who I am.

But watching a client transform their life and become more confident, more peaceful, and just feel lighter as they show up in the world is astounding. I am so grateful to be a witness to that growth and expansion. It inspires me to continue to reflect on who I want to be every day and how I want to show up in my life.

What is the biggest takeaway about the power of coaching to remember?

The POWER of coaching is having continual support. It's always having someone in your corner. It means having someone in your life who can see you, and your situation, clearly and objectively. The POWER of coaching is having someone to hold you accountable and push you when you need it. It means receiving compassion and empathy. You'll always have someone who will acknowledge how far you've come and cheer you on as you reach your goals. The POWER of Coaching is no longer having to go the battle alone. It means walking your path with someone who will be utterly delighted for you as you become more confident, joyful, and abundant in your life.

Are there a few steps or tips you can give someone right now to start them on their transformation?

If you are feeling stuck, anxious, or overwhelmed right now, I encourage you to take one small action. Call a friend, schedule a chat with a coach who you might like, watch a video online, or listen to a meditation. If you are struggling, do something every single day that brings you joy. It does not have to be something huge, and it does not have to cost money. Peruse the shelves of a library or bookstore to see what interests you. Ask someone in your family for more hugs. Stand outside and watch the sun go down. Listen to your favorite music and sing loudly- on your way to work, or dance around your kitchen. When we add joyful moments to our day, we align more and more with our true, authentic self. And THAT is where all the answers lie.

Do you have a gift/session that you can offer us?

If you are ready to reclaim your power, overcome your obstacles, and reach for the stars, then I invite you to have your complimentary 30-minute session with me. Schedule your session on my website: www.AlyssaUtecht.com

About the Author
Alyssa Utecht

Alyssa Utecht is a Transformational Life Coach and Intuitive Guide on a mission to empower women so they can more fully align with their authentic selves. Using her giant toolbox, Alyssa helps clients let go of what no longer serves them and heal what is keeping them stuck, so that they can invite more passion, joy, and ease into their lives. This leads to women showing up more fully and confidently in the world, which is where true healing is found.

Alyssa is a champion for kindness, compassion, and dignity for all. She is an avid supporter of National Parks and her local libraries. She loves reading books, watching comedy specials, and dancing around the kitchen with her family. When she's not assisting others raise their vibe, she loves laughing, having interesting conversations, and sitting under the giant tree where she lives.

What's Next?

Lean In. Let Go. Leap Forward.

What did you think of the stories and expertise that our authors had to share?

Did you learn a few new things that you can take back to your life or work?

Do you now have a better understanding of the power of coaching and how it can be an incredible avenue for transformation in your life and the lives of others?

Did it motivate you to consider being a coach or leveling up as one to facilitate deeper transformations for all those around you?

My hope is that you have a fresh new way of thinking about the coaching industry. If so, please go over to Amazon and leave us a 5-star review!

Our authors were hand-selected for their level of expertise, genuine integrity, and overall level of achievement in the coaching industry. If you enjoyed reading some of their stories and learning about how they help their clients, please take the next step, and reach out to those who inspired you.

Most of the authors in this book speak to groups of all sizes, both in-person and virtually. They also offer products, programs, events, and services that can support you in your life, health, relationships, business/career.

I highly recommend that you take advantage of their special offers, additional downloads, and more when you visit each of the websites listed at the end of their chapters.

In addition, I have put together a website where you can access the author's information to make it easy for you to follow up. There are also more resources on the page about this topic. Go to www.PowerofCoachingBook.com right now, before you forget who you wanted to connect with or find out more about.

Thank you for reading this book. I look forward to bringing you more powerful messages from others in upcoming books, plus more training and teachings in my own books.

If you are interested in becoming a coach in the best way possible, then go to www.AnotherLevelLiving.com/Trainings.

If you are a coach and are interested in becoming an author to have a message to share with the world in an upcoming volume, go to www.AnotherLevelLiving.com/PowerofCoaching. Becoming an author in our book collaborations provides many benefits, which you will discover on the website.

Grab One or More of Free Training Now and Take Your Business and Life to Another Level!

Access the Following Masterclasses:

- The Power of Emotional Intelligence and What It Can Do for You and Your World

- Have You Ever Thought About Being a Life Coach?

- Reclaim the Power of Your Mind and Unlock Your Freedom

- How to Deepen Your Communication with Anyone and Enjoy Being Seen, Heard, and Felt

Get Access Online at: www.AnotherLevelLiving.com/FreeTrainings

Want to Become a Life Coach or Level Up as a Coach?

Become a Certified Life Coach & Emotional Intelligence Expert in Just 4 Days!

This is Our Life Harmony Coach Certification Training Program

Program Benefits

- Start a coaching business right away or scale a current business.
- Expand your capacity & energy as a leader.
- Provide your clients with deep breakthroughs for lasting change.
- Positive impact on self and others around you.

- Increase confidence, energy, & health.
- Breakthrough obstacles and conflicts.
- Cultivate emotional wisdom.
- Improve communication skills.
- Strengthen relationships with ease.
- Reduce stress and increase profits.
- Business & Marketing Expertise Covered.

Learn More at
www.AnotherLevelLiving.com/Trainings

Want to Unleash the Power of Your Mind and Show Others How to Do the Same?

Become a Certified Mind Expert & Neuro-Linguistics Programming (NLP) Practitioner in Just 5 Days!

This is Our Communication Mastery Certification Training Program

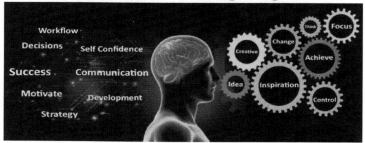

Program Benefits

- Resolve Inner Conflicts.
- Increase Your Confidence
- Be Able to Raise Your Prices.
- Break free from Bad Habits and Limiting Beliefs.
- Operate with More Ease, Grace, & Flow.
- Strengthen Relationships.
- Become the Leader You're Called to Be.
- Gain More Experience & Expertise to Grow Your Biz.
- Facilitate Deeper Transformations.
- Easily Attract & Motivate Your Clients.
- Shift Your Mindset to Receive Your Prosperity.
- Stand Out from Your Competitors.
- Establish Your Own Unique Brand that speaks to your ideal audience.

Learn More at
www.AnotherLevelLiving.com/Trainings

Want to Have More Flow, Faith, and Freedom in Your Business and Life?

Experience a Business Breakthrough Session

Breakthrough to Get to the Root Causes of What's Holding You Back from Having the Business Success and Life Happiness that You Desire and Deserve.

Breakthrough Session Benefits

- Greater Clarity and Alignment on Individual and Business Values
- Align Your Whole Mind, Body, and Soul to Consistently Take Inspired Action and Achieve Goals
- The Removal of Limiting Beliefs and Negative Emotions
- Improved Mental Strength and Resilience
- Faster and Greater Confidence in Decision Making
- The Ability to Access Positive Emotional States Immediately as Needed
- A Quantum Leap in Performance and Productivity
- Bulletproof Self-Confidence
- Increased Motivation and Achievement
- Improved Relationships
- Improved Self and Time Management

Learn more at
www.AnotherLevelLiving.com/Breakthrough

Notes

Notes

Notes

Made in the USA
Middletown, DE
29 August 2024

59863300R00073